NEAT KNITTING TECHNIQUES

—

*How to create
the perfect finish*

—

Jo Shaw

NEAT KNITTING TECHNIQUES

*How to create
the perfect finish*

THE CROWOOD PRESS

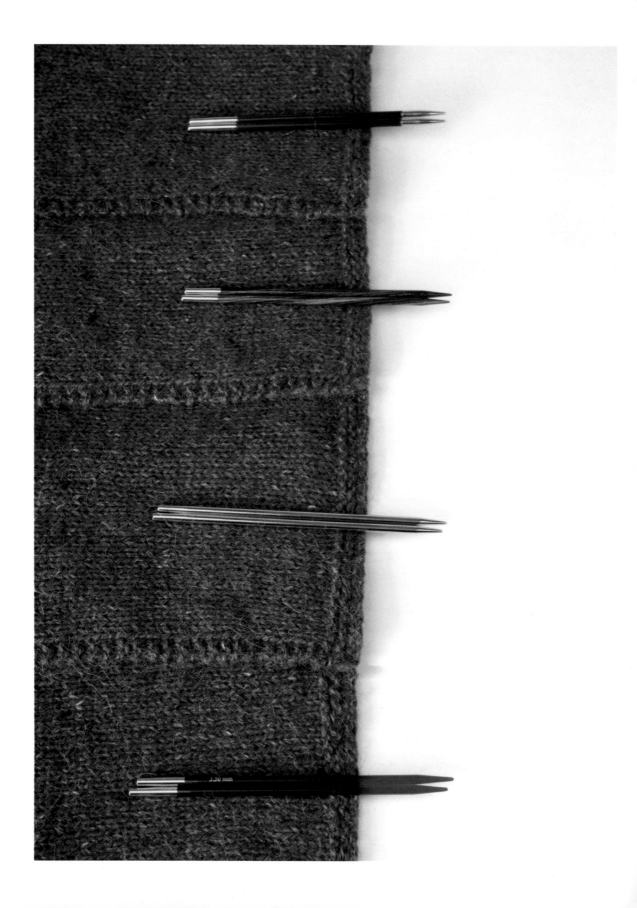

CONTENTS

INTRODUCTION

Knitting has been part of my life for a long time. I'm a knitwear designer, workshop tutor and I've worked in my local yarn shop for quite a number of years. One of my main traits is to research any topic that interests me in as much detail as possible. This led me to complete a Level 3 City and Guilds in Hand Knit Textiles.

I teach workshops and classes on a weekly basis and being able to speak to different knitters and guide them on their knitting journey is rewarding. Many times I have had the wonderful compliment from other knitters that my knitting is 'neat' and this is often followed by 'How do you do that?'. The answer is partly my knitting style, but another good proportion is the techniques and tips that I use to make my knitting neater and easier. My hope, in this book, is to share those with you, so that you too can get the best finish possible from your projects.

It is those finishing touches and details that you add to your project that can be the difference between a project that looks homemade, compared to handmade. It can be very disappointing to put all those hours of knitting into your project and then to find the end result is not how you expected. You'll often hear these called 'finishing techniques'. This definition can be misleading, as it could be interpreted that these methods should be done when you finish; rather, they should be considered before you even start and throughout the entire process. This is why I like to call them 'neatening techniques'. This includes topics that will improve the finishing and neatness of your knitted project. Beginning with your choices before you start, such as swatching and cast-on methods, it also includes techniques within your project that will neaten common issues such as loose knit stitches, joining in yarn, where to work shaping and so on, concluding with sewing seams, blocking and troubleshooting problems.

So if you'll join me, I'll take you through the journey of a project and I'll share these neatening techniques with you.

CHAPTER 1

BEFORE YOU START

CONSISTENCY

Consistency is vital in knitting. Even if you have done something incorrectly or used an inappropriate technique, then if you are consistent, the end result will look right. If something is repeated, then it creates a pattern and it will look like you intended the result. If the result is swapped and changed throughout, then it will look haphazard and messy.

CHOICES

Knitting is a gamut of choices and the best way to be prepared is to be informed; that way you can make the right choice for the finish that you would like.

There are so many different techniques, tools, and yarns out there and they're not all going to suit you. Over many years of experience, I've developed a toolkit for my knitting. This includes my favourite needles, tools, yarns, fibres, and techniques. Yours will most likely differ and I highly recommend that you experiment to find what works for you. All these things improve the finish and neatness of my projects.

So starting at the first item, we have one that is, in my opinion, the foundation of your knitting experience – knitting needles. With your knitting needles, there are many different types, styles, and materials that you can choose from. I'm going to guide you through some of those choices but do experiment and determine which works best for you.

NEEDLES

Straight v. circular

We all have a preference. My opinion is that the only reason that a straight needle outweighs a circular is if you knit with the needle under your arm – although I have taught a number of underarm knitters to use circulars, and it opens so many doors to new techniques and patterns. Straight needles are the traditional choice and that's perhaps because for a long time, circular needles were inferior. The cables would kink and get in the way, the joins between needle and cable were not smooth and it was, generally, an unpleasant experience. However, there are dozens of brands now that produce beautiful, circular needles with non-kink wire and smooth joins.

All three examples show a line of decreases but with variations.

Whatever choice you make at the start of your project, try and stick to it throughout, and the results will be neater.

All the stitches along the decrease line are the same. This is a traditional way of working decreases. As the stitch used is consistent, it looks uniform and intentional.

Alternating ssk and k2tog is not a normal way of using decreases but as they have been alternated consistently, it looks like a pattern and therefore looks intentional and neat.

This sample uses both ssk and k2tog decreases, but at random. This does not look like a pattern and looks far messier than the other two options.

We're discussing neatness though. One big downside to using straight needles is that, as you advance, you have to manage the weight of the project on top of the actual knitting technique. This affects consistency; your knitting style will change as you're having to support the weight of your knitting.

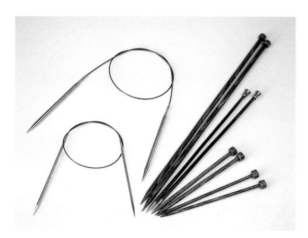

Circular needles are a lot more versatile than straight needles, and they can help keep your knitting more consistent.

Circular needles do not have this issue as the weight of the project is on the cable, which is usually sitting on your lap, and not the needles. This allows the knitting technique to remain consistent throughout the project, plus it is a lot more pleasant and relaxing not to be holding the weight whilst knitting.

Needle material

There are several different needle materials. The most common are metal, wood, bamboo, carbon, and plastic. It's surprising how much the material can affect both the tension and the neatness of your knitting – but it does. It really is worth experimenting to find the material that works best for your knitting technique. The key factor is to keep using the same pair of needles throughout the entirety of your project.

Different materials can suit different knitting styles. My knitting tension tends towards the tight side, so my preference is to use metal needles as the stitches move more smoothly over the needles and that means I am not slowed down as I work.

Using different needle materials can make a vast difference to gauge and the neatness of the knitted fabric.

On the other hand, if you are a loose knitter then a material with a little more surface texture might work better for you, as the stitches will not move around as much.

As a starting point, if you're a tighter knitter, try metal needles and vice versa – if you're a looser knitter, try wood, bamboo, or carbon. This is a generalization and I've known tight knitters prefer wooden needles, but it is a starting point for your own journey to find your perfect needle.

You'll find a preference for a particular needle material, but it may not be the one that makes your knitting the neatest; though it does tend to go hand in hand as the easier ones to knit with will help you be consistent as you work.

As an interesting experiment, I worked several samples with the same yarn, needle brand, and size, but changed the needle material. The gauge on each swatch was slightly different. If I were to make a sweater then there would be a whole dress size difference between the gauges. Needle material does make a difference to the appearance and the size, so stick with the same needles throughout your project.

TOOLS

Stitch markers

Stitch markers are wonderful tools and there are a surprising number of uses for them. They can help you keep on track and be consistent in your project. There are a variety of different forms of stitch markers but there are two types; solid markers and opening ones (though this can also come in the form of split rings).

Try not to use markers that are thick, especially when working with thinner yarns at a tight gauge as the markers can stop the yarn from sitting against the needle and, in some situations, this can create a ladder underneath the marker.

Most uses of stitch markers are to help you recognize a point in your knitting where you might have to do something different, such as start a new round, work an increase, or change to a different stitch pattern. There are other uses that can help with consistency and neatness too. For example, if you are working on a project that requires two matching parts – such as a sweater – you need

Solid stitch markers can only be used on the needle tips.

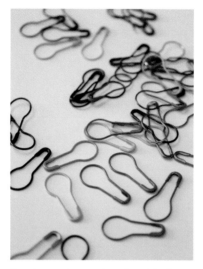
Opening markers, such as French bulb pins, can be used on the needle tips or in the fabric of the knitting.

to ensure the measurement from the armhole to the shoulder is the same on both pieces. Placing a marker at the start of the armhole means that you can either count rows from that point; or if you prefer, measure from it.

Ruler v. tape measure

Should you be using a ruler or a tape measure? The answer depends on the situation. A ruler is going to give you a more accurate measurement compared to a tape measure, as you need to ensure the tape measure is pulled straight. Most of the time in knitting, when we are measuring our work then we don't need to be pinpoint accurate, so a tape measure will be fine for measuring length.

However, the one time that small increments make a difference is when measuring your gauge swatch. That measurement is magnified from our swatch to the stitch count of our project, so any discrepancy on the small measurement will be multiplied. Therefore, when measuring your swatch, use a ruler.

Waste yarn v. stitch holders

When you put stitches on hold to return to at a later point, you can either place these on designated stitch holders, or thread them onto waste yarn using a darning needle. Stitch holders tend to have some weight to them, so they can pull on the neighbouring stitches whilst you're working; plus, you potentially have extra weight to hold whilst you're knitting. You can adjust the stitches later on by giving them a little wiggle with a needle tip, but it saves the trouble if you use waste yarn instead.

Crochet hook

Having a 'rescue' crochet hook in your toolkit can be very helpful. We'll discuss this in more detail in Chapter 8: Troubleshooting, but a crochet hook can be used to fix mistakes. Try to ensure that the size of hook is smaller than the knitting needle size. Firstly, it does make it easier to enter the stitch and, secondly, if the hook is larger then it can pull yarn from neighbouring stitches, thereby distorting them.

Consider the tools that you use, as this can improve neatness.

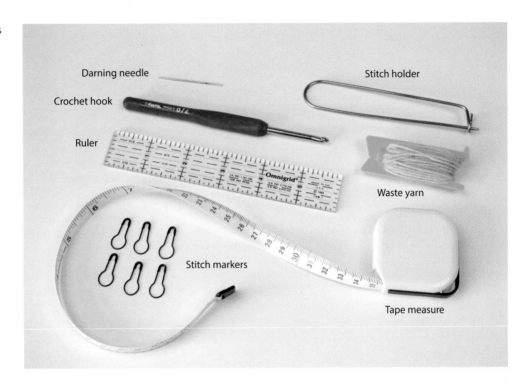

Darning needle

Stitch holder

Crochet hook

Ruler

Waste yarn

Stitch markers

Tape measure

Darning needle

For the same reasons as the crochet hook, ensure that your darning needle is not too large, as it can stretch your stitches. Unless you're using chunky/bulky weight yarn or thicker, then a size 18 or 20 tapestry needle works well.

YARN CHOICES

Choosing yarn for a project can sometimes seem a daunting prospect, as there are so many options. The three factors that make the difference are colour, fibre, and construction.

Colour

For much of the time, your colour choice is just that – your choice. For many projects, it is just about what colour you like or that suits your style. However, there are times when colour can affect the finished item. If the pattern is quite subtle or textured, then a very dark colour will obscure the pattern. After putting in all that effort, it's worth letting it shine by using a colour that will highlight the pattern.

Dye techniques

Apart from using a dark colour for a textured pattern, there isn't much to consider when using a solid colour. However, there are lots of other options on the market, such as semi-solid, variegated, self-striping, speckled and so on. Variegated is the style that I would use with caution. I've been drawn to these beautiful yarns that are a riot of colour, but many times have been disappointed with the finished product. If the contrast between the colours is high, then there are a lot of situations where that colour will hide the beauty of any stitch pattern that you're using.

Semi-solid yarn works well with most stitch patterns and adds a depth of colour to the project.

Speckled yarns are a subtle version of variegated yarn and can work with many stitch patterns, yet add interesting accents to the fabric.

Self-striping yarns save many ends, but the depth of the stripe is affected by stitch count. Using self-striping yarn on a garment could mean that the width is too wide to create stripes.

Consider using variegated yarns with a plain fabric such as garter stitch or stocking stitch. Another good technique is to pair these variegated yarns with a solid colour. This can break up the high contrast and allows the pattern to show.

Contrast

Contrast is important if you are using more than one colour in a project. Contrast is the difference between the colours that you use. If you are working a pattern where the different colours are on the same row, for example, stranded or slipped stitches, then if the contrast is low, you might not be able to see the pattern clearly that you've put all the effort into creating.

Creatively, you might want low contrast for a subtle effect but most of the time, when we are creating a pattern with multiple colours, you'll want it to show clearly. It can be disappointing to put all that effort in then find the colours that you've chosen don't give you the result that you envisaged.

To see whether there is contrast, viewing the yarn on screen in black and white can make it clear. If they look the same or similar in black and white, then the contrast is low. Most camera phones have a black and white filter, so you can take photos and check on your phone. If you don't have access to this, then you can use the squint test. Squint at the yarn and see if they look more, or less, similar.

When I teach contrast in workshops, I lay out a selection of colour combinations and ask my students to choose which they believe would make a good combination. I always try and include one that would look like a contrast such as a grey and red, but their contrast is identical. Invariably, that one tends to get chosen but the finished result wouldn't have the impact that you'd expect.

Using a bright colour with a duller one will not necessarily make it stand out. The colours need to have contrast too. The grey and red yarn viewed in black and white look similar.

EXAMPLES OF CONTRAST IN A PROJECT

When I designed Don't Fret, a music-themed slip stitch shawl, I made two different samples – one has a high contrast and the other has none.

When the images are converted to black and white, the contrast becomes apparent.

A high contrast version of the Don't Fret shawl.

A low contrast version doesn't show the design as clearly but creates a more subtle pattern.

In the high contrast version, the colours look very different to one another.

The low contrast colours look similar in black and white.

Different fibres will give a range of finishes from left to right – wool, alpaca, mohair, cashmere, angora, silk, cotton, linen, acrylic, and bamboo.

There's quite a range of textures within wool; as there are many different breeds of sheep.

Fibre

There are so many fibre choices in yarn. Personal preference comes into play but if you can be informed on the prevailing characteristics of each fibre, then you can make the decisions to get the finish that you want. There are three main types of fibre – animal, plant, and synthetic.

Animal

Animal fibres tend to be warm, since that's the role they play for the animal. Some of the main animal fibres on the market are wool, alpaca, mohair, cashmere, angora, and silk.

- **Wool** is one of the most popular fibres for good reason. It keeps you warm or cool. It absorbs water, yet doesn't feel wet. It can be hardwearing, breathable, elastic, flame retardant, and easy to dye. It blocks beautifully too. It can be superwash-treated, which means that the fibre can be machine-washed. However, this treatment can cause the fibre to stretch and grow once blocked and because of this, I'd highly recommend swatching when using superwash yarn for any project, so you are not surprised by the growth at the end.
- **Alpaca** is very soft and smooth. It absorbs water and keeps you warm. However, it can stretch out of shape and doesn't have the spring back that wool has.
- **Mohair**, from the Angora goat, has a lustre and silkiness, and is temperature-controlling. It is often brushed to create a halo.

- **Cashmere** is from the undercoat of goats (except the Angora) and is a very soft fibre. It is springy and warm and doesn't have a lustre. It is often used in blends because it is so expensive. However, the staple length (the length of the fibre) is quite short, so this means it is not hard-wearing and can be prone to pilling.
- **Angora** is from the fur of the angora rabbit and is very soft and can felt easily, so you have to treat it with care.
- **Silk** is the exception, as it is reeled from the cocoons of the silkworm, rather than shorn as with other animal fibres. Silk has a very high tensile strength but doesn't abrade well. It can have a high shine, good drape and is temperature-controlling.

Plant

The main two plant fibres on the market are cotton and linen. There are others such as hemp and nettle, but these aren't as common. Even though bamboo and other cellulose-based fibres, for example, banana, soy, corn and so on come from a plant; they are produced in a very different way and it's more appropriate to include these in artificial fibres. Plant fibres are ideal, if you don't want stretch and need to stay cool.

- **Cotton** conducts heat away from the body, which is good for hot climates, but this means that it is a poor insulator. It is a heavy and curly fibre and these fibres can straighten in wear due to its own weight pulling it down. However, upon a warm wash and dry, it can shrink back to the original size. Cotton has little elasticity and will wrinkle easily. It also has a tendency to pill.
- **Linen** is the strongest plant fibre. It is cool to the touch. It absorbs moisture, including perspiration, which makes it a good fabric for hot climates. It is easy to wash. Linen does not pill and will become a better fabric with age.

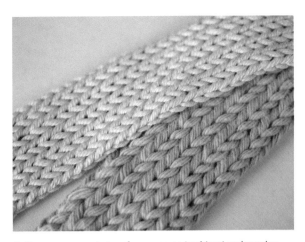

Cotton yarn comes in two forms; mercerized (top) and regular (bottom). Regular cotton is the natural texture and has a matt appearance. Mercerized yarn is chemically treated to create a stronger yarn with a shine.

Acrylic can be produced to mimic other fibres, so the construction and finish can vary widely.

Synthetic

The three most used synthetic fibres are acrylic, nylon, and viscose. Artificial fibres are cheaper, durable, and machine-washable.

- **Acrylic** is effectively plastic, so it will keep you warm but it is not breathable, so it can quickly lead to perspiration. It is machine-washable but be careful about introducing heat near it, as it may melt. Acrylic is often included in blended yarns, as it will reduce the cost.

- **Nylon** is strong and durable. It is rarely, if ever, used on its own but it is included in blends to improve the durability of yarn. Many sock yarn blends include nylon to improve the longevity.
- **Viscose** is produced from plant sources such as bamboo. Bamboo-sourced viscose produces a soft yarn. The finished fabric has good drape and often has a lustre.

Blends

Many yarns are blends of fibres. This means that you tend to get the best characteristics from each fibre. For example, if the yarn was 55 per cent wool, 33 per cent acrylic and 12 per cent cashmere, then the majority of the fibre is wool and you'll get wool's beneficial properties, such as temperature control and elasticity, but the acrylic content will most likely make it more machine washable and cheaper. That small proportion of cashmere will add a buttery softness to the yarn. Blends do give you the best

of both worlds. Just remember to check what the majority of the yarn is, as those are the properties that will prevail.

YARN CONSTRUCTION

There are numerous different types of yarn construction, but the most common type is plied yarn. Other types, such as chain, tube, tape, bouclé, slub and so on, will give a less traditional and more textured fabric.

Ply

Talking about yarn ply can be confusing, as there is a traditional yarn weight system that uses the term 'ply'. You might have heard of 2-ply, 4-ply, or 10-ply yarns. Traditionally, the number of plies in the yarn was the same as the thickness, but yarn manufacture has changed and now you can get a single-ply yarn that is a chunky/bulky weight or a 4-ply yarn that is aran.

BEST USES

Imagine you are planning a cardigan project; your choice of yarn depends on which stitch pattern is being used and which factors are important to you. Here are a few examples:

- If it had a textured stitch pattern, then you would use a yarn with good stitch definition and a colour that showed clearly, such as a worsted-spun wool blend in a mid to light colour.
- If it was lacy, then drape would be important. A 2-ply silk yarn would work well.
- If it's plain and going to be worn a lot, then a long-lasting fibre would be best, such as a non-superwash wool yarn.
- If it's to be worn to stay warm, then best to stick with animal fibre. A wool/alpaca blend would be a good choice.
- If it's for a baby, then being able to machine wash would definitely be a good idea. Most acrylic blends are machine washable.

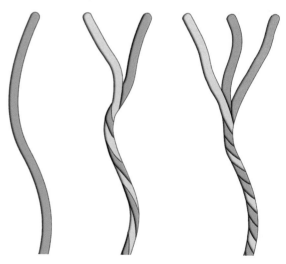

The structure of different plied yarns makes a difference to the finished fabric. From left to right – single, 2-ply and 3-ply yarn.

Left to right – single, 2-ply, 3-ply. In stocking stitch, single ply yarn can create a bias in the fabric, if the twist in the yarn isn't balanced; 2-ply yarns create an uneven fabric; 3-ply tends to create a smoother fabric.

Left to right – single, 2-ply, 3-ply. Lace knitting works well for all types of yarn but 2-ply lends itself, as its construction allows the holes to open more.

Yarn is constructed of different numbers of plies. Some yarns will have a single-ply, or 2 or 8. The number of plies does affect the characteristics of the yarn and some will give a better finish for certain projects.

Single-ply yarns have one main strand and can't be split. This can give an elegant definition to the stitches but it can, sometimes, lead to a bias (twist) in stocking stitch. This type of yarn can also lead to frustration in casting on. Depending on the direction of spin, then the cast-on can 'unspin' the yarn and it can break apart. If you have this problem, either stop every few stitches and twist the yarn the other way, or use a different cast-on, for example, swap a cable cast-on for a long-tailed or vice versa.

Two-ply yarns have two strands spun together. This gives more balance to the yarn, so it won't bias. It has more strength because of the extra ply. It's a perfect match for lace knitting, as the plies will move into each other and open up those yarnovers. However, it will give an uneven texture to stocking stitch.

Left to right – single, 2-ply, 3-ply. Single ply yarn has good stitch definition, though it can be a little flat; 2-ply yarns give a soft edge to stitch patterns; 3-ply yarns give the best stitch definition.

Three (or more) ply yarns have three strands spun together. This creates a round yarn and the more plies, the rounder the yarn. This allows good stitch definition, so will work well for texture, stocking stitch and cables. However, it will close the holes more in lace knitting.

KNITTING STYLES

One of the key elements of our knitting that affects the neatness is how we actually knit. When I learnt to knit, I just picked up the yarn and swung it around the needle in the English style. I managed to perfect this to be quite quick but after many years of this, my hands started to object to my grip on the yarn and it became a painful process. In *The Principles of Knitting*, June Hemmons Hiatt recommends having a few different ways of knitting in your toolkit. The one caveat that I would add is it does affect the consistency in your knitting. If possible, stick to the same technique throughout a project, but sometimes comfort overrides style.

I re-taught myself a different knitting style (a form of flicking) that allowed my fingers to be more relaxed. The upside of this change was I became faster, more consistent and resulting from both of those factors, my finished knitting became neater.

There are several different knitting styles. I get to witness many knitters in my classes, and all the little variations that we have fascinate me. Even within the same style of knitting, we might have the yarn over a different finger, tensioned in a different way, or our hands at a different angle. If you've not had the benefit of seeing others knit, then you might wonder what these other styles are.

English (also known as throwing)

English knitting involves holding the yarn in the right hand and moving the hand to take the yarn around the needle. English style tends to be the most common method, especially for those self-taught, but it can be slower and less consistent than other techniques, as the hands have further to move.

Continental (also known as picking)

The yarn is held in the left hand and the right-hand needle tip is used to pick the yarn through the stitch. This can be a very quick method for the knit stitch. Continental purling is slower to work than the knit, as there is much more movement needed. The Continental style is a common technique, especially for those that are taught by European knitters. It is a good starting point, if you are already a crocheter, as the yarn is held in a similar way.

English knitting requires a lot of movement by the right hand to create the stitch.

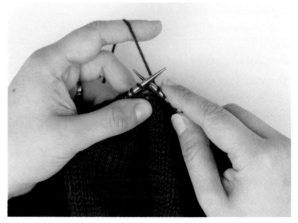

Continental knitting tends to be a quick method, as the movements to create a stitch are small.

Flicking (also known as lever)

This is effectively a variation of English style, but the hand does not leave the needle. Instead, the finger is flicked forwards around the needle.

There are other variations of this method that require the needle to be anchored. Underarm or armpit knitting has the end of the needle trapped under the arm. In the Shetland Islands, a knitting belt is used to prop the end of the needle at the waist. Both allow the hands to concentrate on just making the knitting stitch, thereby speeding up the process.

My knitting style is a form of flicking but with the hands held above the needle.

Flicking comes in many different forms. One of the most common is to hold the needles from underneath the knitting.

Portuguese (also known as Incan)

The yarn is anchored from the left. This is done by either the use of a pin attached to the left shoulder, or the yarn is taken around the back of the neck. This is quite a localized technique and is more popular with knitters from Portugal and Latin America.

The Portuguese purl is a lot easier and quicker to create than the knit stitch.

Combination

Combination knitting is a mixture of Eastern and Western knitting and uses the Continental knitting style. It is a lot easier to work continentally a purl stitch in the Eastern manner because you can just scoop the yarn through without moving your left hand. No matter what your knitting style, you always enter the stitch through the right leg. Therefore, combination knitters must compensate on subsequent rows for the stitch sitting in a different position, so the knit stitch will be worked through the 'back loop'.

Improving neatness

Irrespective of your technique, there are improvements that you could make to increase neatness. This stems back to consistency. The more consistent your technique, the neater your finished knitting will be. The key to consistency is to reduce your movements and keep a consistent rhythm. Having the right needle material will assist this (see earlier in this chapter). Experimenting with needle material and style not only improves neatness, but can also be gentler on your hands.

Reducing movement can be an issue for English-style knitters, as your hand comes off the needle. If you're an English-style knitter, see if you can master one of the other styles. Just remember, mastering a new technique will not happen overnight.

The other factor in improving neatness is working correctly with your knitting needles. If you don't, then this leads to loose or tight tension and both can create inconsistent stitches. An ideal technique involves the stitch on the left-hand needle moving onto the tapered part of the needle and when the right needle tip is inserted, this needle remains touching the left-hand needle until it removes

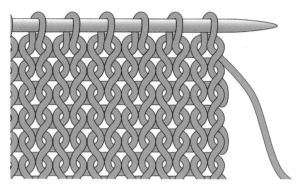

All the previous styles are examples of Western knitting, where the stitch has the right leg at the front of the needle.

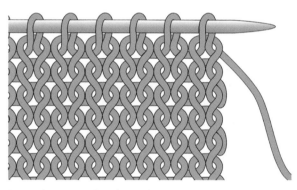

Eastern knitting is when the stitch is sitting on the needle with the right leg of the stitch at the back.

the stitch. The stitch is then sized on the full part of the right-hand needle and not the tapered tip. Sizing your stitches on the tapered tip can create inconsistency in your fabric, since the stitch will be a different size depending on which part of the taper it is worked. This is often what happens with tight knitters. Conversely, loose knitters don't keep the needle tips together the entire time that a stitch is made; you can identify when this happens as there is a gap between the base of the stitches and the bottom of the needle.

SWATCHING

Many knitters don't like making swatches. Since your finished swatch has no other purpose than to tell you a couple of numbers, it can be perceived by some as a waste of time. However, those numbers make the difference between a well-fitting project and one that's destined for the back of the cupboard. Considering the amount of time that we invest into our projects, surely it is worth that little extra time to make a swatch and get the finish that we wish to create.

How to swatch well

You might have heard others say that their swatch was inaccurate. Sometimes, this is due to changing your knitting style as you relax into your project, or the weight of all the yarn has affected the tension in the finished project; or the swatch wasn't an accurate representation in the first place. The point of your swatch is to be able to see what a section of your knitted fabric would look like. In an ideal world, a swatch the size of your project would be the most accurate, but no one is going to intentionally do that.

Imagine if you cut a big section of your fabric out of the finished project. That is what you're trying to achieve in your swatch. This means that you don't want any factors affecting your tension. The cast-on and cast-off need to have no restriction, that is, they need to be loose. Adding garter stitch to the sides of your swatch allows it to lie beautifully flat, but it can distort your gauge. Ideally, you don't want any edge treatment. I do tend to add two garter stitches on the sides of mine, as a nod to trying to keep it flattened a little, but I compensate by making sure my swatches are larger.

At first glance, it makes sense to cast on the number of stitches mentioned in the gauge of the pattern and see if it measures 10cm (4in). This will be so inaccurate that it really isn't worth doing. Most of your edge stitches will not be the same gauge as the centre part of your knitting, so the outer 2.5cm (1in) on each side needs to be ignored. The bigger the swatch, the more accurate the measurement. The minimum width of a swatch is 15cm (6in) but ideally, you want to make them larger. My preferred size is 20cm (8in).

Making a swatch

Let me guide you through a swatch. The pattern is asking for 22 stitches and 28 rows in 10cm (4in). Make sure you use the exact same pair of needles that you intend to knit the project with.

- Cast on 20cm (8in) of stitches, for example, double the stitch gauge, so 44 stitches in this situation. Make sure you use a loose cast-on method.
- Knit 2 rows.
- **Row 1 (RS):** knit.
- **Row 2 (WS):** k2, purl to last 2 sts, k2.
- Rep Rows 1 and 2 until work measures 15–20cm (6–8in).

For later reference, it is useful to mark into your swatch which needle size was used. Sometimes, you will see this done at the start of the swatch but the yarnovers will distort the following rows, so to avoid that, work this at the end of the swatch. On the final RS row, add in pairs of yarnovers (yo) and knit two togethers (k2tog) to indicate full mm size and purl stitches to indicate any decimal size. In other words, start your row as follows:

3mm – k4, (yo, k2tog) three times, knit to end.

3.5mm – k4, (yo, k2tog) three times, (k1, p1) twice, knit to end.

- Rep Row 2 once.
- Knit 3 more rows.

Either cast off loosely or cut the yarn to twice the width. If you've cut your yarn, use a darning needle and thread the end through all the live stitches (as if placing them on waste yarn). This stops the cast off restricting the edge.

How to measure your swatch

Measure your swatch when it's just off the needles and make a record of this gauge; that way you can check your project as you work on it to see if there's any change in tension. However, to compare it to the pattern gauge, it needs to be wet blocked (see Chapter 7 for how to block). With a swatch, don't use any pins, just let it dry flat.

If the project is going to contain a lot of yarn, for example, if you are making a garment or blanket, it is a good idea to hang your swatch for a few days with something weighing the edge down, such as pegs. Just make sure the swatch is thoroughly dried. Most fibres will still contain moisture but will feel dry to the touch, so give it a few days to dry.

When your swatch is dry, lay it flat. Using a ruler (not a tape measure), measure a 10cm (4in) square in the centre of the swatch. Count how many stitches and rows are in this square and that is your gauge. Make sure you count any quarter- and half-stitches, as these will affect size too.

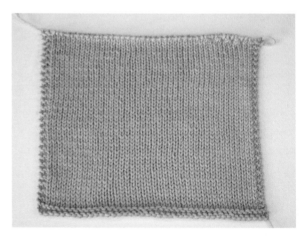

An accurate swatch needs to be large enough that the edges and sides do not distort the gauge reading.

Hanging a swatch allows you to see if the added weight of the yarn in the project will change the gauge measurements.

When measuring a swatch, you can use pins to mark where you want to measure from.

Stitch patterns

Some patterns will not tell you what the stocking stitch gauge should be; instead it will only list the gauge in pattern. The principle is the same as a stocking stitch swatch, but just change the stocking stitch for the required pattern.

When measuring, repeat the same method as before, block and then measure out a 10cm (4in) square.

The double moss stitch in this swatch isn't too difficult to count the stitches.

EXAMPLE MEASURING GAUGE FOR A COMPLEX STITCH PATTERN

The issues happen when it is a more complex pattern and it's not obvious how to count the stitches, such as in this lace swatch.

You'll be able to tell how many stitches and rows are in a pattern repeat, as it will be in the pattern. You can then use a little bit of maths to change your numbers to match the gauge in the pattern. In this example, there are 21 stitches and 18 rows in a pattern repeat that measures 7.5cm (3in) width by 5cm (2in) high. Work out how many stitches this would be in 2.5cm (1in) by dividing the stitches by the measurements; then multiply by the required gauge.

For example, 21 stitches divided by 7.5cm and 18 rows divided by 5cm = 2.8 stitches and 3.6 rows in 1cm (½in). Multiply by 10cm (4in) and the gauge of the swatch is 28 stitches by 36 rows in 10cm (4in).

For complex stitch patterns, mark out a full pattern repeat with pins and measure the width and height.

Swatching in the round

When making a swatch, you're replicating a small part of your project. If your project is worked flat, then make the swatch flat but if you're working in the round, then make the swatch in the round. When working stocking stitch in the round, you aren't working any purl stitches and these tend to be a little larger than their knit counterparts. This means that if you swatch flat for a project in the round, then the gauge is likely to be inaccurate. There are a couple of techniques for swatching in the round.

Working a swatch completely in the round does waste time and yarn, since half of the swatch won't be needed.

Strand method

A quicker method is to work your swatch on circular needles, but used flat. Knit a row of your swatch and then push the stitches back to the opposite end to where your yarn is. Stretch out some excess yarn across the back of the swatch and start knitting again. Repeat this for every row.

One downside of this technique is the yarn cannot be used again and sometimes, when quantities are tight, you might want to reuse the yarn in the swatch.

When finished, the strands across the back can be cut and the swatch will lie flat.

This method works well for stranded colourwork, though the outer edges will be inaccurate.

Loop method

The other method is worked in a similar way on circular needles. Knit a row of your swatch and push the stitches back to the other end. Measure out your yarn to four times the width of your swatch and work a row with the strand across the back (not the end that is attached to the ball). Once this row is complete, push the stitches to the other end again. Repeat these steps until the swatch is the desired size.

The loop method leaves an untidy edge that will not give accurate measurements, so ensure the swatch is large enough to compensate.

CHAPTER 2

FIRST STEPS

CAST-ONS

Which cast-on?

There will be some projects where the cast-on choice does not matter as it will not be visible when finished. However, many projects have a visible cast-on and if that edge is wavy, restrictive, or untidy, it can detract from the look of the piece.

From my experience of speaking to a lot of knitters, it's quite interesting to see how many are amazed that there's more than just 'their' way of casting on. There are literally hundreds of methods and they could fill a book all of their own. There are many that can be used for regular knitting but there are some that have very specific uses, such as sock toes, provisional cast-ons, and so on. Unless you know all the cast-on methods, then it could be overwhelming to make that choice.

Workhorse cast-ons

We all have our 'go-to' cast-on; the one that you fall back on. I like to call them the 'workhorse' cast-ons, as they will help you out in most situations with faithful service. The three cast-on methods that I would define as 'workhorse' cast-ons include cable, long-tailed and twisted German. You might have another that you tend to use, but these three are the most common. If in doubt about which cast-on method to use, choose one of the 'workhorse' cast-ons.

Cable cast-on

The knitted cast-on is often the method taught to beginner knitters. It is easy to work and replicates the normal knit stitch, so it is easy to remember. However, it is not a cast-on that I find useful. By inserting the needle into the stitch, it creates loose and untidy edges and it is one of the slower cast-ons to work.

This flow chart can guide you through the choices for some of the most common types of cast-ons.

Start

Do you need a workhorse cast-on? These will work for most situations

— Yes → Cable / **Long-tailed** / Twisted German

— No ↓

Do you need a provisional cast-on?

— Yes → Do you have a circular needle in the right size?
  — Yes → Provisional using circular needle
  — No ↓
  Do you have a crochet hook?
  — Yes → Chained **Provisional Crochet**
  — No → Waste Yarn

— No → Are you starting from the centre out?

Are you starting from the centre out?
— No → Do you need a double-sided cast-on e.g. are you making toe-up socks?
  — Yes → Judy's Magic / **Turkish**
  — No → Disappearing Loop
— Yes → Are you Möbius knitting?
  — No → (up to Are you starting from the centre out?)
  — Yes → Möbius

A workhorse?
— Yes → Cable / **Long-tailed** / Twisted German
— No → Are you starting with ribbing?
  — Yes → Do you need a stretchy edge?
    — No → Alternating Cable / **Alternating Long Tail**
    — Yes → Channel Island / **Estonian** / Twisted German / **Tilly's Very Stretchy** / Tubular
  — No → Do you need a decorative edge?
    — Yes → Channel Island / **Estonian** / Lace / **Picot** / Two-Colour / **Turned Hem** / I-Cord
    — No → How about a cast on for buttonholes?
      — No → (loops back)
      — Yes → Backward Loop / **Cable** / Twisted Backward Loop / **Slip Knot** / Buttonhole

Instead, I'd recommend the cable cast-on, which is an improved version of the knitted cast-on. It is created in the same way but instead of inserting the needle into the stitch, it is inserted between the stitches. This creates a decorative twisted edge and it is neater as it hasn't stretched the stitches open.

For a neater corner finish, before placing the final stitch onto the needle, bring the yarn to the front between the needles.

The cable cast-on creates a decorative and neat edge.

This is a slight variation on the cable cast-on where, at step 3, the stitch is placed on the needle by rotating the RHN clockwise and inserting the LHN from left to right. This twists the edge giving a fuller, more pronounced finish.

STEP-BY-STEP: CABLE CAST-ON

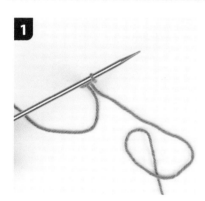

Step 1. Start with a slipknot on the needle.

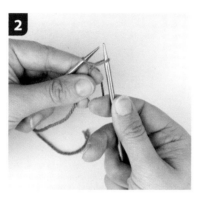

Step 2. Insert the RHN into the loop on the LHN and knit a stitch without removing loop from LHN.

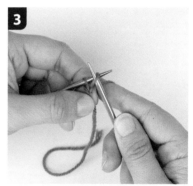

Step 3. Place stitch onto LHN without pulling tight (so it is easy to insert the needle in the next step).

Step 4. Insert RHN into gap between the stitches and under the LHN.

Step 5. Knit another stitch.

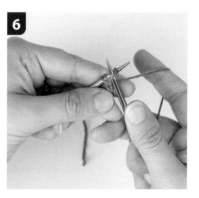

Step 6. Place stitch onto LHN and repeat from step 4 until all stitches are cast on.

Slingshot hold

There is a large section of cast-ons that are created with the yarn in the slingshot hold. This allows for good tension and greater speed. A slingshot hold will always require a long tail of yarn to be measured out. There are lots of different methods to work out how much yarn that you need, such as wrapping the yarn around the needle or test knitting a section, but it doesn't need to be over-complicated. My rule of thumb is to measure out 1cm (½in) per stitch for yarn up to DK weight and 2.5cm (1in) per stitch for yarn that is thicker, plus an extra 15cm (6in) for the tail. Just err on the side of extra yarn.

Once you've measured out your long tail, make a slipknot and place on the needle. Most of the time it doesn't matter which side the ball is on, but if you happen to have a colour change at the slipknot then ensure the upper thread is attached to the ball.

When using the slingshot hold, the cast-on created will be the right side of the work; therefore, the next row, ideally, needs to start on a wrong side row.

STEP-BY-STEP: SLINGSHOT HOLD CAST-ON

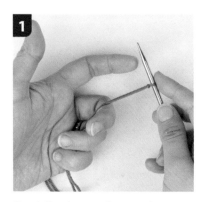

Step 1. Keeping your finger on the slipknot, so it doesn't fall off the needle, palm both strands in your left hand.

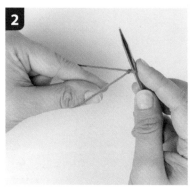

Step 2. Pinch your forefinger and thumb together and place between the two strands.

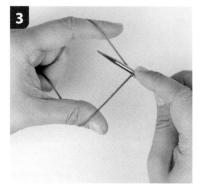

Step 3. Open your forefinger and thumb out.

Step 4. Point them towards the ceiling.

CASTING ON A LARGE NUMBER OF STITCHES

If you have hundreds of stitches to cast on, it's a lot easier to use two balls or opposite ends of the yarn to create the cast-on instead. Just create a slipknot with the yarns held together. This does mean there is an extra two ends to darn in, but it stops the frustrating scenario of nearing the end of the cast-on only to discover that you've run out of yarn.

Long-tailed cast-on

There are two different methods for creating this cast-on. The English method, where each yarn end is held in separate hands; and the Continental method, where the yarn is held in the slingshot method. The step-by-step shows the Continental method as it is quicker to work but both produce the same results.

The long-tailed cast-on is a quick and neat method, plus it allows for a gentle stretch at the edge.

STEP-BY-STEP: LONG-TAILED CAST-ON

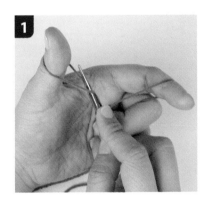

Step 1. Once in the slingshot hold, insert the needle into the loop on the thumb from below.

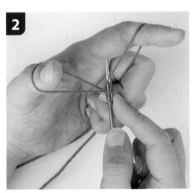

Step 2. Take the needle over the top of the thread on the forefinger.

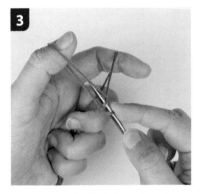

Step 3. Scoop this back through the loop on the thumb.

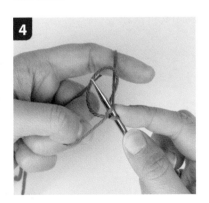

Step 4. Remove the thumb from the loop.

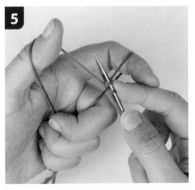

Step 5. Reinsert the thumb into the thread and pull to the left.

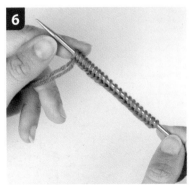

Step 6. Repeat steps 1–5 until desired number of stitches are cast on.

Twisted German, also known as Old Norwegian
This is my preferred method. It's a form of long-tailed cast-on with a twist – literally. It's created in exactly the same way, but the initial loop on the thumb is twisted to add a little extra structure and stretch to the edge. This is perfect for sock cuffs, as it stretches out but springs back into shape too.

The twisted German cast-on gives an elastic edge that is easy to work into on the next row.

STEP-BY-STEP: TWISTED GERMAN CAST-ON

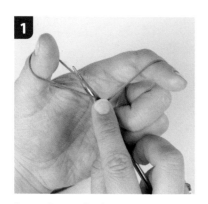

Step 1. Once in the slingshot hold, insert the needle under both strands on the thumb.

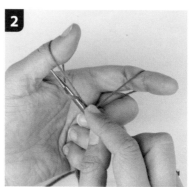

Step 2. Take the needle down into the loop on the thumb and bring back to the centre position.

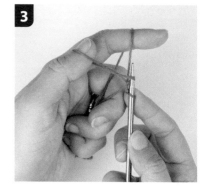

Step 3. With the needle still through this loop, take the needle over the top of the thread on the forefinger.

Step 4. Scoop this thread back through the cross created by the thumb loop.

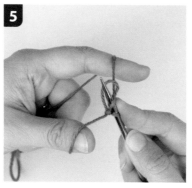

Step 5. Remove thumb from the loop and reinsert into the thread and pull to the left.

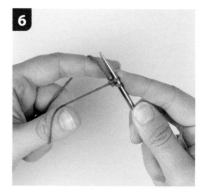

Step 6. Repeat steps 1–5 until desired number of stitches are cast on.

Cast-on toolkit

You have your 'workhorse' cast-on but you might want to change it up for a more decorative edge or for a specialized technique. Here are a handful of useful cast-ons to have in your toolkit.

Estonian cast-on

It gives a decorative edge that's elastic and is a variation of the long-tailed cast-on.

The Estonian cast-on works well with 1 × 1 ribbing and seed stitch.

When used with 2 × 2 ribbing, the Estonian cast-on creates a decorative wrap around the base of the ribbing column.

ADJUSTING YOUR CAST-ON

Some projects will require more stretch at the cast-on than others, for example, socks, hats and so on. There's a standard practice that suggests casting on over two needles to make the edge stretchier. This does work but at the expense of neatness. The other downsides are that this causes the stitches to be loose on the needle and if joining to work in the round, it makes it hard to stop twists from happening, as the stitches have a tendency to spin around the needle.

The better practice is to space out the cast-on stitches on your needle. Keep each stitch a fingertip apart. By using your finger to space the stitches, then you can place them evenly and easily. This gives you control with the stretch too. Place them nearer together for a tighter edge and further apart for more stretch.

This cast-on creates the right side of the work. If working flat, start with a wrong side row. If working in the round, don't use the swap stitch method to close the round as the wrong side of the cast-on will be on the outside.

STEP-BY-STEP: ESTONIAN CAST-ON

Step 1. Start with a slingshot hold, but move the thumb position, so you come up from under the thread instead.

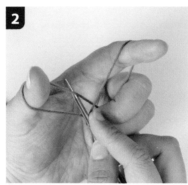

Step 2. Insert the needle under the upper thread on the thumb.

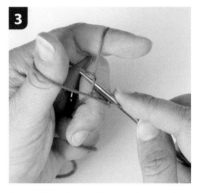

Step 3. Take the needle over the top of the thread on the forefinger and scoop this back through the loop on the thumb.

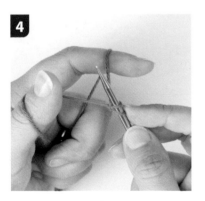

Step 4. Remove the thumb from the loop and reinsert the thumb into the thread from above and pull to the left.

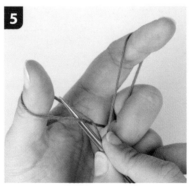

Step 5. In the traditional slingshot hold, work the next stitch as a long-tailed cast-on stitch, that is, work steps 1–4 of long-tailed cast-on.

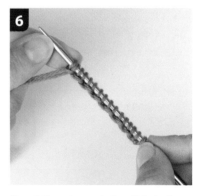

Step 6. Repeat steps 1–5 until desired number of stitches are cast on.

Provisional crochet cast-on

There are several methods for provisional cast-ons, including just using waste yarn and working a few rows in stocking stitch before starting to work the pattern. My favourite method is to work a crochet chain over a knitting needle. The benefits to this method are it is quick, and easy to undo at the end – the crochet chain can just be unravelled. The crochet hook size doesn't matter, as this chain is removed later. Using something similar in size to your knitting needle is a good starting point though.

Start working in your main yarn and follow the pattern instructions. See Chapter 5: Edges for details on how to return provisional stitches to your needles.

A provisional cast-on is used when you need to return to this edge at a later point; either to knit in the opposite direction or to seamlessly join to another edge.

STEP-BY-STEP: PROVISIONAL CROCHET CAST-ON

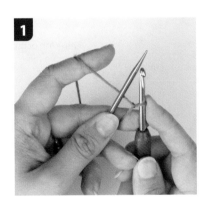

Step 1. Using waste yarn, place a slipknot onto your crochet hook. Hold the yarn in your left hand with the knitting needle over the strand.

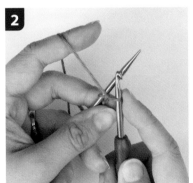

Step 2. Use the hook to scoop the strand from the left-hand side of the yarn and through the loop on the hook.

Step 4. Repeat steps 2–4 until you've cast on all but the final stitch. The final stitch is the loop on the hook; move this to the knitting needle.

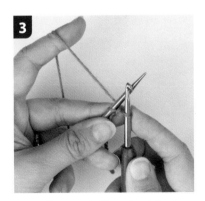

Step 3. The strand will now be sitting in front of the knitting needle – move this behind the needle.

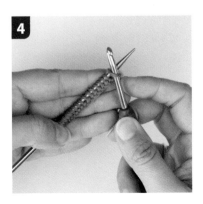

1 × 1 tubular cast-on

There are numerous methods for creating a tubular cast-on. This is the method that I find the easiest and neatest. It does alter slightly depending on whether it's an odd or even stitch count; or working in the round or flat. The initial cast on can be done with any method, or use the provisional crochet chain cast-on and it will be easier to remove the waste yarn later. If the final stitch count is even, cast on half the number of stitches, plus one. If the stitch count is odd, add one to final stitch count and cast on half this number. Cast on this number with waste yarn and your main needle size.

The tubular cast-on creates a rolled edge that looks very professional. This method only works with 1 × 1 ribbing, although there are alternatives for different types of stitch patterns.

- **Set up row:** Using the main yarn and needle three sizes smaller than the needle instructed in the pattern, purl a row.
- **Next row (RS):** *k1, insert LHN from front to back into running thread, p1 through this thread, rep from * until last stitch (if odd), then k1; or last 2 sts (if even) and then k1, insert LHN from front to back into running thread, purl thread and final stitch together.

Working in the round
- Join for working in the round.
- **Round 1:** *sl 1 wyib, p1, rep from * until end; or if odd, end with sl 1 wyib.
- **Round 2:** *k1, sl 1 wyif, rep from * until end; or if odd, end with k1.
- **Round 3:** Rep Round 1.

Working flat
- **Row 1 (WS):** (if odd, start sl 1), *k1, sl 1 wyif, rep from * until end.
- **Row 2 (RS):** *k1, sl 1 wyif, rep from * until end; or if odd, end with k1.
- **Row 3:** Rep Row 1.
- Change to larger needles and continue pattern as instructed.

When the cast-on has been completed, cut the waste yarn and gently remove; or simply undo, if the provisional crochet method was used.

Judy's magic cast-on

This is far easier to work using circular needles rather than double-pointed needles. If you prefer another type of needle, then you can easily move to your preferred type after completing the cast-on.

Judy's magic cast-on is only used when working in the round. It creates a closed cast-on with live stitches all around. This is perfect for creating toe-up socks.

STEP-BY-STEP: JUDY'S MAGIC CAST-ON

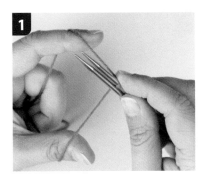

Step 1. Measure out a long tail. Holding the knitting needles together throughout, place the yarn over the back needle with the tail end at the top.

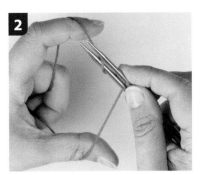

Step 2. Using the slingshot hold and keeping a finger on the loop on the needle, rotate the needles, so the bottom needle goes over the top strand, then the thread goes between the needles and return to centre.

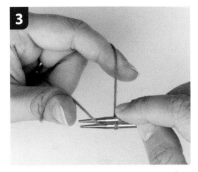

Step 3. Rotate needles so that they straddle the bottom thread. Point to the floor, then towards yourself and back to centre.

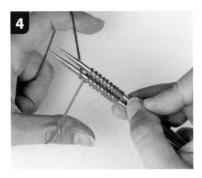

Step 4. Repeat steps 2 and 3 until one less stitch is cast on. Repeat step 2 once more.

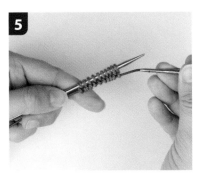

Step 5. Hold on to the threads, so the stitches don't come off. Point your needle tips to the right. Remove the bottom needle by pulling to the right.

Step 6. Follow your pattern as instructed and start working in the round.

Disappearing loop cast-on

Instead of casting on a small number of stitches and then sewing the hole closed later, this method gives a neat and easy option for centre-out knitting.

The disappearing loop cast-on is ideal for working from the centre out, such as a circular blanket or a top-down hat.

STEP-BY-STEP: DISAPPEARING LOOP CAST-ON

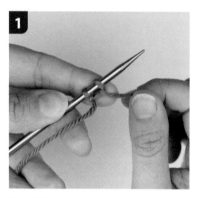

Step 1. Place a slipknot on the needle. Create a backward loop and place on the needle, with the working yarn ending at the front.

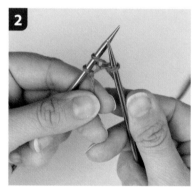

Step 2. Working into the same backward loop stitch throughout, knit one.

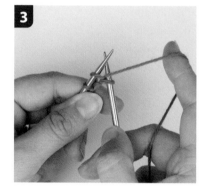

Step 3. Work a yarnover by bringing the yarn to the front under the needle, and then anticlockwise over the top.

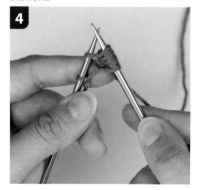

Step 4. Repeat Steps 2 and 3 until the required number of stitches are cast on the RHN (don't include the slipknot or backward loop in your count).

Step 5. Remove the slipknot and the backward loop from the knitting needle; undo the slipknot and pull the end to close the loop.

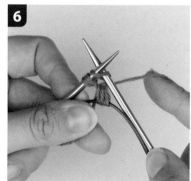

Step 6. Split stitches evenly over your needles and start working in the round as instructed.

PURL STITCH PROBLEMS

Purl stitch can cause quite a number of problems in our knitting, though you might not always realize that is the cause. When a purl stitch is created, it uses slightly more yarn than its knit counterpart. This means that the purl stitch can be slightly larger.

Rowing out

For some knitters, this can be so pronounced that it causes an effect called 'rowing out'. Rowing out happens when creating stocking stitch flat.

This happens simply because the purl stitch is larger than the knit. There are several different solutions that can be used to combat this. If the effect is very pronounced, then using a smaller needle on the purl rows can help, or use the combination purl mentioned in Chapter 1. However, these just cover up the problem and don't fix it. Ideally, to prevent rowing out, try to increase the tension on your purl stitches. There are a couple of techniques to think about:

- Try wrapping the yarn an extra turn around a finger to add tension.
- Make sure that the needles are always touching until you've completed your purl stitch.
- After completing each purl stitch, give the yarn a little tug to tighten it up.

Edges

This same problem shows itself in the left-hand edge of stocking stitch. It's an issue that most beginner knitters come across. After turning to the wrong side, for the first 2 stitches, keep the tension on the yarn and pull those stitches tight. This will keep it the same length as the other side.

When 'rowing out', the knit stitch rows are neat and tidy but the purl rows are slightly larger.

This can be more apparent on the reverse and causes distinctive lines on the back of the work.

The left-hand edge will be longer than the right. This is caused by those purl stitches.

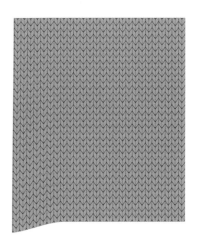

Ribbing

Ribbing can be a problem for those who like their knitting to be neat. 1 × 1 ribbing has those gaping knit stitches and in wider ribbing that final knit stitch before any purl stitch will be loose. This is caused by that loose purl stitch, so we need to tighten it up.

Tighten purl method

The 'tighten' purl technique is an easy one to implement. Every time that you change from a knit stitch to a purl stitch, take the yarn to the back of the work between the needles and pull the yarn back tightly, then continue in pattern (just keep the tension on until completing the next stitch). This works easily for 1 × 1 ribbing, as you can k1, p1 and take the yarn back to pull it tightly and then you're in position for your next knit stitch.

There's an extra step when working a wider rib. For example, when working 2 × 2 ribbing, after taking the yarn to the back of the work to pull that first purl stitch tight, you need to take it back to the front again to purl the next stitch. It is worth doing but can slow you down a little.

Combination purl method

The other technique is the 'combination' purl technique. When changing from knit to purl, work the first purl with combination knitting, that is, purl by taking the yarn clockwise around the needle. This shortens the amount of yarn used in the stitch. However, the stitch is sitting in the Eastern orientation on the needle and the stitch needs to be worked through the back loop on the following row to ensure that it doesn't become twisted. Having to perform a second half of the method on subsequent rows can be a big downside, as it is easy to forget. However, since the stitch is sitting in a different position, it does jog the memory.

The last knit stitch before a purl can be open and loose.

The tighten purl method works well and is the easier of the two options to work.

The combination purl method gives the best results but is a more involved technique.

If working this technique in the round then repeat this every time that you change from knit to purl but remember to insert the needle through the back loop on subsequent rows, that is, from the back from left to right. If working flat, when returning on the wrong side to the stitch that was combination purled, knit this through the back loop but wrap the yarn clockwise around the needle when knitting this stitch.

Twisted ribbing
When working 1 × 1 ribbing, neither method creates perfectly neat ribbing. If you're still not happy with the finish, then change the ribbing stitch pattern.

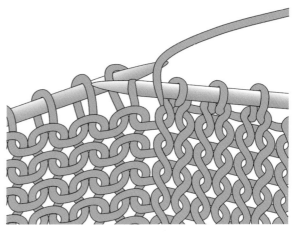

On the subsequent RS rows, insert the needle as if to purl through the back loop and then combination purl again.

The simplest method to change to is twisted ribbing, for example, k1 tbl, p1. This is easy to work in the round but remember to p1 tbl, k1 on the wrong side, if working flat.

The WS can be worked in k1, p1 but this will give a different stitch pattern – the half-twisted rib, which has a more zigzag effect.

Yarnovers are used in lace knitting to create the holes. A normal yarnover is created by taking the yarn anticlockwise around and over the needle and finishing where the yarn is needed for the next stitch. It's most common to work these with knit stitches on either side but, sometimes, yarnovers will be surrounded by purl and knit stitches. There is a situation where this combination can lead to different-sized yarnovers and the thicker the yarn, the more obvious this difference can be.

When the pattern is knit, yarnover, purl, then the yarnover will be larger than the opposite – purl, yarnover, knit. This is a similar issue to purl stitch problems. It happens because the yarn must travel a little further when going from knit to purl and this creates a larger hole. Often, these are paired in a pattern and the difference in size can be very apparent. It is not always the case, so this isn't a technique that needs to be utilized every time this stitch combination happens. Use the following solution, if you're not happy with the yarnover sizing.

The solution is to work the yarnover by taking the yarn clockwise around the needle. This is similar to the combination purl method, except it is a yarnover in this case. This means that you must remember to work into the back loop of the yarnover on subsequent rows, so it doesn't twist and close the hole.

When working a knit to purl yarnover, these can be larger than other yarnovers, as seen at the bottom right of the centre motif.

Working a knit to purl yarnover clockwise creates more evenly sized holes.

WORKING IN THE ROUND

Working in the round offers a lot of benefits. It cuts down on seams, makes the instructions simpler as there is no wrong side and reduces the amount of purling needed, which works particularly well for colourwork knitting and stops 'rowing out'. However, there can be a few areas where neatness can be affected.

Joins between needles

It depends on the type of needle being used for circular knitting. Using a single circular needle in the round stops any joins between needles and is the neatest method, but this doesn't always work well on small circumferences, such as socks. There are small circular needles which work well, but they can be an acquired taste. It isn't possible to work smaller areas such as toes with these needles and this requires a different needle type to be used.

Double-pointed needles (DPNs), two circulars or one circular used in the magic loop method are the most common methods. However, all these techniques mean that there will be a point in the round where you need to change from one needle to another, and these join points can lead to issues with neatness.

Ladders
There are several methods to combat this.

- If using DPNs, then pull the first and second stitch on each new needle as tight as possible and this will pull the ladder in.
- If your round has any purl stitches, ensure the needle join ends with a purl stitch and starts with a knit stitch.
- If all else fails, move the join a couple of stitches every few rounds and this stops the ladder building up.

Ladders can develop between the needles. This is where there is either a loose stitch or a loose gap between two stitch columns.

Tight joins

Another issue can happen when using two circular needles or magic loop is tight columns of stitches. This happens because at the joins the last stitch worked is on the cable and not the needle, so if the yarn is pulled tight at this point, then the stitch is sized to the cable and not the needle. This can make it difficult to get the stitches back onto the needle and creates a tight column of stitches.

This one takes more practice to achieve. It's about getting your tension 'just right'. Try to keep the cable with the stitches just worked close to the start of the next needle, so the yarn doesn't have far to travel and when pulling the yarn, try to make sure the last stitch is the same size as the others.

Tight columns of stitches at the joins can be a subtle difference. The looser the gauge, the more apparent this can be.

Keep the cable close to the needle when changing needle. This helps to maintain the correct size of the stitch on the cable.

Joining in the round

The other area where neatness is affected is when joining the stitches in the round. If you don't do anything, then there will be a gap in the cast-on. Subsequent rows can have long strands at the join, so just ensure that you pull the first stitches on the subsequent round to close this gap.

K2tog method

Cast on an extra stitch and, when joining in the round, slip the stitch with the working yarn to LHN and knit the first and last stitches together using both the working yarn and the cast-on tail to close the gap. Just remember to work the first stitch that has used both yarns as one stitch when returning to it on the following row.

Swap method

This is my preferred method. When joining in the round, swap the position of the first and last stitches on the needle. Just make sure that you move the initial cast-on stitch first. The final stitch is attached to the working yarn, so has some movement to go over the first stitch.

When there are gaps at the join, these can be closed when darning in the end, but there are a couple of techniques that you can use instead.

The k2tog method is easy to work but not the neatest of the two options.

The swap method gives the neatest join but just remember to move the initial cast on stitch first to make it easier to work.

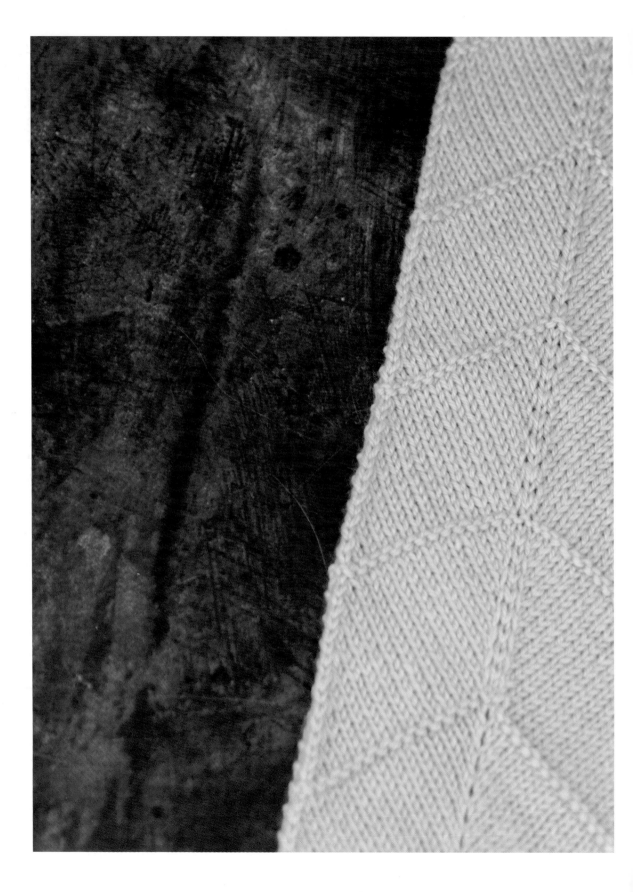

CHAPTER 3

SHAPING

SHAPING CHOICES

When it comes to knitting patterns, there's a lot of variation in writing style. An independent knitting designer such as myself, is not restricted as much by space, so I have the freedom to explain the detail in my patterns. However, when the design is for a magazine or a pattern house, then the writing style needs to be more succinct to fit into the limited space available for the instructions. This means that some details are left to the knitter to decide. Often, shaping instructions lack detail. For example, a pattern will tell you to decrease at each end of the next row. However, it doesn't tell you where or which decrease to use. These choices make a difference to the finished look and can affect the neatness too.

Soft or hard line?

Often, decreases are worked in pairs. The right-leaning decrease will be 'knit two together' (k2tog) and the most common left-leaning decreases will be either 'slip, knit, pass stitch over' (skpo) or 'slip, slip, knit two together' (ssk). The left-leaning decrease is a common issue for neatness and this is discussed further on in the chapter, but for now, let's assume that your decrease pair is k2tog and ssk.

These samples replicate a sleeve decrease line. Depending on the order that the decreases are worked, there's quite a difference in the look of the piece.

Having the ssk on the left and k2tog on the right of the central line gives a hard vertical line, which gives a cleaner finish.

Alternatively, with the ssk on the right and k2tog on the left of the central line gives a softer, more feathered finish.

Just be aware that positioning depends on how the garment is constructed. For example, if working the sleeve flat, the ssk will be worked on the right edge and the k2tog on the left edge to give the hard line finish.

Positioning

So you've decided which decrease is going in which position. The next choice is to decide where to place the decrease at the edge. There are three common choices – on the edge, 1 stitch in or 2 stitches in from the edge. They all have their pros and cons and ultimately, it depends on what you want the project to look like.

On the edge

This gives a soft edge, but there are a few downsides to consider. If working in the round, placing paired decreases directly next to each other means that they will pull apart from each other and look untidy. However, if working flat and placing that decrease at the edge, you will be making it harder for yourself to get a clean finish. When working decreases on a flat piece, the edges will either be sewn together, or picked up and a band knitted on. In both situations, you will have to work around the decreases in that edge stitch. This will make it more difficult to be consistent and create a clean finish.

One stitch in from the edge

This positioning prevents the problem with picking up or sewing, as you will have full single column at the edge to work with. However, the issue of the decreases pulling away can sometimes leave a small gap at this edge.

Two stitches in from the edge

If this suits the project then this is, normally, my preferred choice. You get the same benefits of 1 stitch in from the edge, that is, it's easy to create a neat seam or band. However, you also avoid the downsides of the 1 stitch in. As there is a stitch between the decrease line and the edge, you don't have that 'gapping' issue.

This technique is called 'fully fashioned' as the decrease line becomes part of the finish, as it is clearly visible. Obviously, this can be part of its downside as the decrease is on display in the project, but it looks neat and clean.

Placing the decrease on the edge stitch allows the decrease to be hidden in the seam or edging.

Placing the decrease 1 stitch in from edge makes it easier to pick up stitches or sew the edges together.

When the decrease is 2 stitches in from the edge, you avoid the downsides of the other positions, but the decrease is clearly on display.

DECREASES

As I mentioned earlier, decreases are worked in mirrored pairs. The k2tog is a right-leaning decrease and because of its construction, it creates a neat stitch. However, the left-leaning decrease is not as neat. There can be a gap between the decrease and the stitch to the right of it. This can look like a ladder. The line can look untidy, as it has a zigzag effect and the stitches themselves can look larger than the surrounding ones. The reason this happens is because it's the left stitch of the decrease that is tightened up when the following stitch is worked. With the k2tog, this stitch is on top, so it looks neat, whereas with a left-leaning decrease, the left stitch is hidden underneath and the excess yarn moves into the visible stitch; hence the untidy decrease. There's never quite a perfect left-leaning decrease but there are lots of options that improve the finish.

Different left-leaning options

Slip, knit, pass over (skpo)
This is not a perfect match to k2tog. There is a zigzag and the stitch underneath is enlarged. The skpo is created by slipping the next stitch knitwise, knitting one, then passing the slipped stitch over.

Knit two together through the back loop (k2togtbl)
It twists the front stitch creating a distinctive zigzag and creates a cross at the base of the stitch. It is created by inserting the needle through the back loop of 2 stitches and knitting them together.

Slip, slip, knit (ssk)
This has a slightly longer process but gives a tidier finish than the skpo. However, it still has a small zigzag and is prone to creating a ladder on the right-hand side. It is created by slipping the next 2 stitches knitwise one at a time, then knitting them together through the back loop (the easiest method is to leave

The most traditional left-leaning decrease is the skpo. It's very easy to work.

The k2togtbl is the easiest option to work but it is also the untidiest version.

For many modern patterns, the ssk seems to be the most popular version of left-leaning increase used.

the slipped stitches on the RHN and insert the LHN needle into the front legs of the slipped stitches, from left to right and then knit them together).

Cat Bordhi has a useful technique for reducing the ladders on the right-hand side of a left-leaning decrease. This technique requires a setup row. On the previous round to the decrease, slip the stitch before the ssk purlwise. When returning to it on the next round, use the strand slipped on the previous round to knit this stitch, then work the ssk.

On the following round, work the stitch prior to the ssk in the same manner by using the slip strand to work the stitch. If you work the ssk through the back loop on this row then this stops the zig zag effect too. Continue in this manner by always working the stitch prior to the ssk with the slip strand until all decreases have been worked. To get that stitch prior to the ssk back into normal knitting, knit with the slip strand, slip back to the LHN and then knit it with the working yarn.

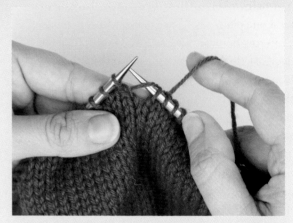

Treat the slipped stitch as a dropped stitch by slipping the stitch to the RHN, then picking up the strand with this needle and passing the stitch over this strand, then reorientate the stitch, so the right leg is at the front.

Slip knitwise, slip purlwise, knit (ssk)

Instead of slipping both stitches knitwise, slip only the first knitwise and the second purlwise before knitting them through the back loop. This creates a slightly flatter stitch with less zigzag.

Knit two together left (k2tog-L)

This technique has a more involved process but is an improvement on the previous methods. This decrease is created without slipping stitches. Insert the RHN knitwise into the first stitch then purlwise into the next. Rotate the RHN slightly to the back to pull excess thread out of the front stitch into the back stitch. Knit these 2 stitches together but only remove the LHN from the first stitch. Use the LHN to pull the left-hand stitch in order to pull all excess to the back, then drop from the LHN.

The slip knitwise, slip purlwise, knit is a small variation on the normal ssk.

The k2tog-L is an improvement on the previous decreases because it deals with the excess yarn moving into the front stitch.

Knitting through the back loop on the following row

Normally, when working decreases, there is at least one plain row between each decrease. On the plain row following the decrease, knit the previous decrease through the back loop. This technique can be paired with any of the above increases to improve the straightness of the line.

Slip, yank, twist, knit (SYTK)

This method, developed by Techknitter, gives a good match for a k2tog. To work this decrease, slip the first stitch knitwise, insert the RHN purlwise into the next stitch and stretch that stitch by pulling the needle tips away from each other, twist the yanked stitch clockwise (by removing from the needle and replacing) so that the stitch crosses with right leg at the front, return the first stitch to the LHN and knit the stitches together through the back loop. The downside to this method is the extra steps can slow down the rhythm and speed of the knitting.

Comparing left-leaning decreases

All the techniques have their pros and cons. Unfortunately, it seems to be that the neater the technique, the longer and more complex the process. Balancing ease with neatness, my preference is to work k2tog-L paired with the k-tbl on the following row. However, I would not use this with lace knitting and would instead use a standard ssk, as any method that slips the second stitch purlwise could potentially close yarnover holes on the row below.

Knitting through the back loop on following rows can solve the zigzag problem.

The SYTK gives a neat straight line even without adding the ktbl on the following row.

On the following plain row, knit the decrease stitch
from the previous row through the back loop to
reduce the zigzag effect.

Step 1. Insert the RHN knitwise into the
first stitch.

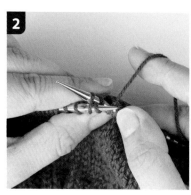

Step 2. Rotate to insert RHN purlwise into
the next.

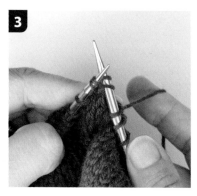

Step 3. Rotate the needle slightly to the
back to remove excess thread out of the
front stitch.

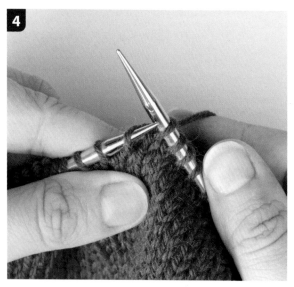

Step 4. Knit these 2 stitches together but only remove the LHN
from the first stitch.

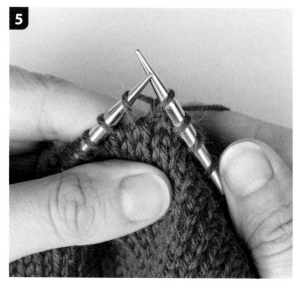

Step 5. Use the LHN to pull the left-hand stitch and bring all
excess yarn to the back then drop from LHN.

DECREASING ALONG A CENTRAL LINE

There are certain circumstances where decreases are placed directly next to each other. Sometimes, this can look a little untidy as the stitches pull away from each other creating a gap between the decreases. If you don't like the look of how the decreases are placed, you can add a stitch or two between the stitches or change the decreases to a centred double decrease instead.

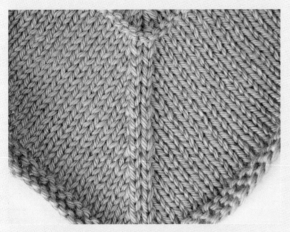

This sample is worked k2tog then ssk. This can look neat but if this was on an item that required stretch, such as a sock, then a gap appears between the decreases.

This sample is worked ssk then k2tog. This has the same issue. A gap can appear between the decreases.

Slip 1, k2tog, pass slipped stitch over creates a soft central line and can be swapped for a k2tog and ssk directly next to each other.

Slip 2, k1, pass slipped stitches over creates a beautiful neat knit column.

INCREASES

Increases raise the same questions about placement and choice as decreases. Knowing how the increases look in relation to one another can be helpful. There are several different choices for increases. There are four different increase types that I will use – make one, lifted increases, backward loop, and knit front and back. The first three can easily be substituted with each other as they are all worked by creating a stitch between stitches. The knit front and back uses a stitch to create another, so if altering a pattern to substitute a kfb or vice versa, then just remember that any instructions will have to be changed to account for the one extra or less stitch worked.

Make one increases

'Make one increases' are created by working into the bar between stitches. This means that the neighbouring stitches can be distorted.

The order of the increases also makes a difference to appearance. The top two samples are worked in the order, m1r then m1l, giving a neat central column.

'Make one increases' can be tricky to work as the strand that they are worked into is twisted, so it can be very tight to get your needle tip into the stitch. This is one problem that I see repeatedly; since it can be difficult to work, then it often makes more sense to the beginner knitter to work into the easy side of the stitch. If you do this then you'll get a big hole, as you are effectively working a yarnover. I find myself repeating in workshops that if you find a 'make one increase' easy to get a needle into, then you're probably doing it wrong! Since these increases are a little slower to work, I will often substitute these for a quicker version, if it's practical.

When 'make one increases' are worked either side of a single stitch, both increases pull on that central stitch which causes it to have large stitches on the increase row and smaller stitches on the plain row.

Working 2 plain stitches between each increase reduces this pull as the increase only pulls on one side of the neighbouring stitch.

If the increases are worked in the order, m1l then m1r, then the central stitches have vertical strands running down the side of the centre.

STEP-BY-STEP: MAKE ONE LEFT INCREASE

Step 1. Insert RHN from back to front into strand between needles.

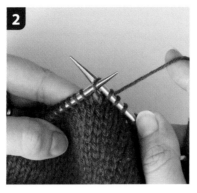

Step 2. Insert LHN from left to right into this strand ending with LHN at the front.

Step 3. Knit this strand.

STEP-BY-STEP: MAKE ONE RIGHT INCREASE

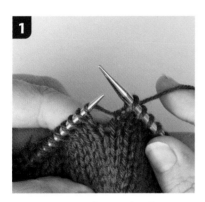

Step 1. Insert LHN from back to front into strand between needles.

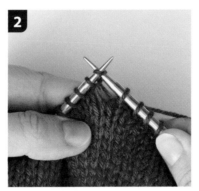

Step 2. Insert RHN knitwise into this strand. This is very tight, so roll the thread forwards on the needle to give yourself room.

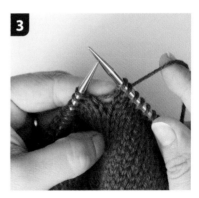

Step 3. Knit this strand.

Lifted increases

Lifted increases are my preference when it's practical to use them. Instead of working into the strand between the needles, you are working into the stitch below the one on the needle. This means it's not as tight and you aren't twisting anything, so it's easy to work and can create quite an invisible increase. Again, the order of increases makes a difference to the look.

However, if the increases are on every row then this increase will only work using them in the order, LLI then RLI. If worked in the opposite order, then you will be working into the same stitch on every subsequent row and it just won't work.

LLI, k2, RLI. Working the LLI then RLI gives those same vertical strands that happen with the 'make one increase'.

RLI, k1, LLI. This order gives a neater finish, but it ideally wants to have at least 2 stitches between, otherwise it creates a little hole. This can be used as a design feature, but it is slightly harder to work too.

LLI, k2, RLI. This order gives the same vertical strands but the central stitches are more even.

RLI, k2, LLI gives an extra finishing touch for a top-down garment, as this has the added benefit of looking like a single knit column from upside down.

STEP-BY-STEP: LEFT-LIFTED INCREASE

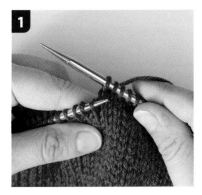

Step 1. Insert LHN from back to front into stitch two below the one on the needle.

Step 2. Insert RHN into this stitch that was lifted to LHN from front to back.

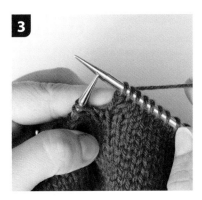

Step 3. Knit the stitch.

STEP-BY-STEP: RIGHT-LIFTED INCREASE

Step 1. Insert RHN from back to front into stitch below the stitch on LHN.

Step 2. Place this strand onto LHN by inserting from left to right and remove RHN and reinsert into this stitch knitwise.

Step 3. Knit the stitch.

Backward loop increase or make one away/towards

This is an easy increase to work. However, it does have quite a big downside. It has a little gap at the base of the stitch. In stocking stitch, this can look quite blatant, so I tend to use this with more open fabrics such as lace knitting where the small hole isn't apparent. It can still be used with stocking stitch, but the previous two increases give a more invisible finish. The order makes a difference to the finished look.

The other downside is that the 'make one away' is easy to work but the mirrored 'make one towards' has a second step on the following row. The loop will be sitting differently on the needle, so it jogs the memory but I am often reluctant to recommend techniques that have this second row step as it is so easy to forget.

Both backward loop increases are made using loops in the working yarn. This can just be manipulated into a loop and placed on the needle, but it's easier to wrap the yarn around a finger in a specific manner and then place it on the needle, as described in the following step-by-step guides.

M1a, k1, m1t leaves an untidier central column with the vertical strands similar to the other lifted increases.

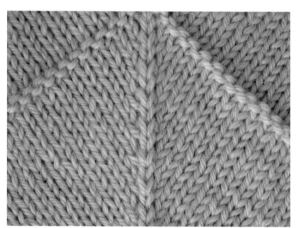

The recommended order is, m1t, k1, m1a, as it gives a neater central stitch.

STEP-BY-STEP: MAKE ONE AWAY INCREASE

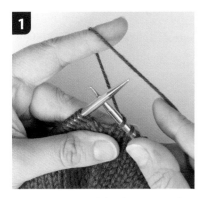

Step 1. Using the left forefinger, wrap the working yarn anticlockwise around finger starting from underneath.

Step 2. Insert RHN from right to left into strand and place onto needle.

STEP-BY-STEP: MAKE ONE TOWARDS INCREASE

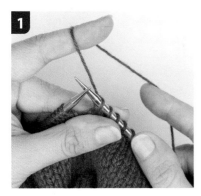

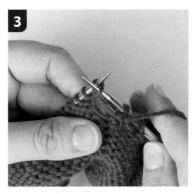

Step 1. Using left forefinger, wrap the working yarn clockwise around finger starting from above.

Step 2. With RHN to the left of working yarn, insert from right to left into this strand and place onto needle.

Step 3. This will be sitting as in the Eastern mount on the needle, so on the following row, work into the back loop of the stitch.

Knit front and back

This is worked by knitting into the front then back of the stitch. This is easy to work and is often one of the first increases that a knitter learns. It is not one that I often use, as the increase creates a purl bar, so it is obvious to see in a sea of stocking stitch. It can be useful in garter stitch though, as the purl bar blends in well with the other purl bumps.

It is more difficult to mirror too. The mirror takes a few extra steps to work, but the second kfb can always be worked 1 stitch earlier, so the purl bump sits in the same place.

As you can perhaps tell, I'm not the biggest fan of the kfb. There's quite a bit of fuss around getting the mirror or the placement right, especially when the pattern doesn't give you guidance in the first place. It's far easier to place a make one or lifted increase into a pattern and they give a far more invisible increase too.

The kfb is worked before the mirrored version and gives a narrow central band.

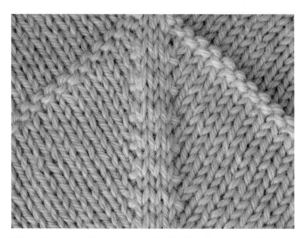

When the mirrored version is worked before the standard kfb then the central band appears wider.

To eliminate the purl bump, the kfb can be worked by knitting into the front of the stitch and instead of working into the back, the back strand is slipped instead.

STEP-BY-STEP: KNIT FRONT AND BACK INCREASE

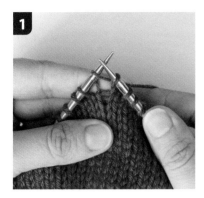

Step 1. Knit into the stitch without taking it off the left-hand needle.

Step 2. Knit into the back of this same stitch.

Step 3. Remove stitch from LHN.

STEP-BY-STEP: KFB MIRRORED INCREASE

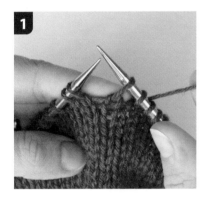

Step 1. Slip stitch knitwise.

Step 2. Return to LHN and then knit stitch and remove from LHN.

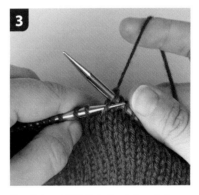

Step 3. Insert LHN into front strand of stitch below RHN from left to right and knit this through the back loop.

SHAPING IN PATTERN

The principles are the same whether you are increasing or decreasing, but I'm going to describe the methods with just decreasing for efficiency. It is easy to work out shaping at the end of the row, since you can just repeat the stitch pattern until you run out of stitches. However, the beginning of the row is not as simple. It does depend on what type of stitch pattern you are working, as several factors need to be considered.

Knit and purl

Shaping in pattern becomes quite easy once you can 'read' your knitting. If you can recognize what stitch you worked on the previous row, then it's quite simple to work out what it should be on your current one. However, it takes time and practice to learn this. In the meantime, stitch markers can be very helpful. Place stitch markers between the first few stitch pattern repeats. You can use these markers to work backwards in the pattern.

On row 9, there are 7 stitches to work, so start the pattern repeat 7 stitches from the end of the pattern repeat. You can use either the charted or written instructions, though it is easier to work from the chart as you can just count 7 squares in, whereas, you'd have to read the entire instructions to work this out in the written instructions.

If you don't have or want to use stitch markers, then it's a matter of keeping track of the decreases. If you've decreased 4 stitches along your edge, then start the instruction 4 stitches in.

Colourwork knitting, such as stranded, intarsia and mosaic knitting can all use this method. When the knitting pattern uses more than 1 stitch at once, there are more aspects to consider.

Cables

The general rule of thumb when shaping in pattern is if you can't work the full stitch instructions, work them in the same stitch pattern as the base fabric. This will most likely be stocking stitch or reverse stocking stitch, but it could be other patterns such as moss stitch, garter stitch and so on.

In this sample, the left-hand shaping is just swapped for stocking stitch, whereas the right-hand side is changed for smaller cables.

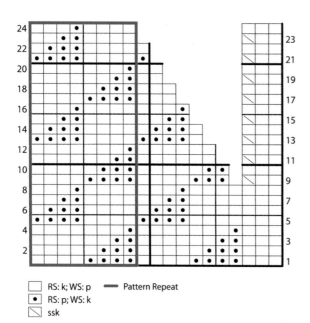

	RS: k; WS: p	▬	Pattern Repeat
•	RS: p; WS: k		
◺	ssk		

In this charted example, the stitch repeat is 8 stitches. Once you get to a point where you can't work a full repeat at the edge, see how many stitches are left between the marker and the decrease.

If you use this principle with cables and they encompass a large number of stitches, then it can look quite odd having all the cables stop and the edge having a mass of stocking stitch. Instead, you can change the cable.

In the cable chart, on Row 23, the 3/3 LC cannot be worked as it needs 6 stitches, but there are only 4 available. Instead of working in stocking stitch, as I've done on the left-hand side, work a different cable instead. Try to maintain the top part of the cable if possible, that is, the stitches that cross at the

front. The original cable has 3 in front and 3 at the back. Since I only have 4 stitches, I'm going to work a left cross cable with 3 stitches at the front and only 1 at the back. On Row 19, there aren't enough stitches to maintain the 3 stitches at the front, so I'm going to drop this to 2 and hold only 1 at the back.

It sounds strange that I'm changing the pattern so much, but as you can see in the sample, the right-hand side looks like a part of the cable has been decreased off, compared to the left-hand side that looks like it's just changed to stocking stitch.

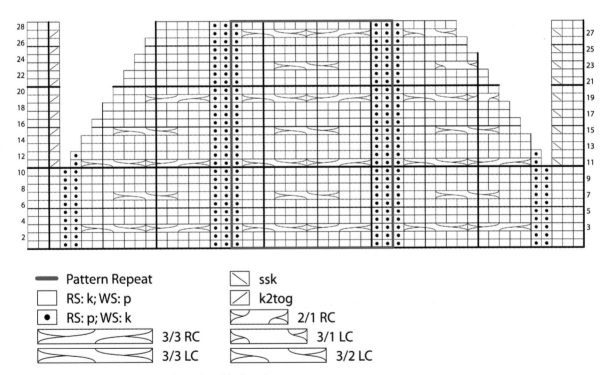

	Pattern Repeat		ssk
	RS: k; WS: p		k2tog
•	RS: p; WS: k		2/1 RC
	3/3 RC		3/1 LC
	3/3 LC		3/2 LC

This chart of the cable sample shows how the cables have been swapped for versions that use fewer stitches.

Lace

Shaping with lace knitting has the potential to go wrong. Lace knitting is pairing increases and decreases together to create the holes, so when removing stitches at the sides, these pairs need to be maintained otherwise the stitch count will change more than intended.

You don't need to worry about the entire row of knitting. Use your stitch markers on the repeats and just concentrate on the pattern repeat that doesn't have the full number of stitches and make sure that each increase has a matching decrease. If it doesn't, then work that stitch as a knit stitch instead. That principle will work to keep your stitch count correct. However, if you want to get the best finish then you can take it a step further and see if you can alter anything to keep the pattern working to the edge.

When decreasing in lace, every k2tog or ssk must have a matching yarnover. If a centred double decrease such as s2kpo is used, there should be 2 matching yarnovers as the s2kpo decreases 2 stitches.

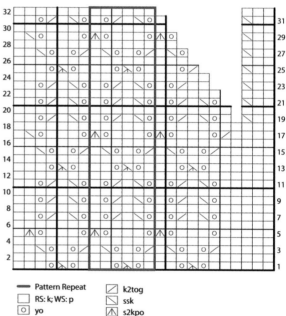

▬▬ Pattern Repeat	☑ k2tog	
☐ RS: k; WS: p	☒ ssk	
⊙ yo	⋀ s2kpo	
⋈ sl 1-k2tog-psso		

For example, on Row 25, there aren't enough stitches to work the s2kpo and keep the stitch count correct. However, I could change this to a k2tog and yarnover pair instead. This will keep the eyelet pattern and the stitch count correct.

SHORT ROWS

Short rows can be useful to create 3D shapes in your knitting. The Nimble sock pattern (see Chapter 9: Projects) uses short rows to shape the heel of the sock. The traditional method for working a short row is to use the 'wrap and turn' method. This involves wrapping the working yarn around the base of a stitch and turning to work in the opposite direction. Later, when returning to this wrapped stitch, the wrap will be picked up to close any gaps; however, this wrap can be easily overlooked.

Using the German short row method instead means that it is difficult to overlook the wrap and turn stitch as it sits as a double stitch on the needle. It has the secondary benefit of being easier and quicker to work too. When altering patterns from traditional wrap and turn, work the w&t stitch in pattern then follow the instructions below.

In this short rows sample, the short rows are worked in pink using German short rows.

STEP-BY-STEP: KNIT SIDE SHORT ROWS

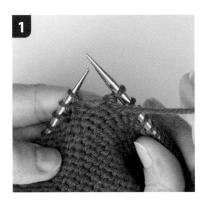

Step 1. After working the stitch in pattern, turn work and slip stitch purlwise to RHN.

Step 2. Take working yarn up and over to the back of the RHN. Pull tight to bring the stitch up. It will look like a double stitch on the needle.

Step 3. Take yarn from back between needles to the front. Pull tight and continue in pattern.

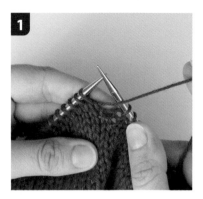

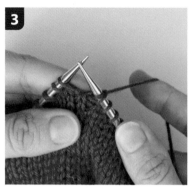

Step 1. After working stitch in pattern, turn work and take working yarn between needles to the front.

Step 2. Slip stitch purlwise to RHN.

Step 3. Take yarn over the top of RHN and pull tight to create double stitch. Continue in pattern.

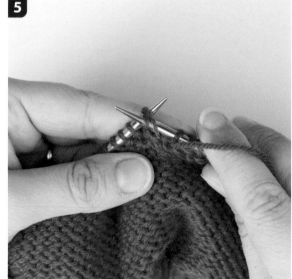

Left to right – Double stitch on right side, double stitch on wrong side. When you return to these stitches on subsequent rows, treat the double stitch as one stitch and work into both strands.

PROBLEMS WITH PURL SIDE SHORT ROWS IN THE ROUND

Purl side German short rows look the same as the knit side, when the double stitch is worked back in from the wrong side. However, there are neatness issues if worked in from the right side.

Luckily, there is a technique to fix this issue. Work the purl side short rows as normal but when returning to them to knit the double stitches, don't knit each double stitch together. Each double stitch consists of two strands.

If working in the round and the wrong side double stitches are worked from the right side instead, then small holes form. This doesn't necessarily look bad as it is consistent, but the knit side doesn't have these holes.

After using the technique described, then the result is much neater.

Step 1. At the first double stitch, knit just the first strand.

Step 2. Knit the first strand of the next stitch with the remaining half of the first double stitch.

Repeat this until the final double stitch and knit the remaining half together with the next normal stitch to maintain the stitch count.

CHAPTER 4

WORKING WITH MORE THAN ONE YARN

JOINING IN YARN

Joining in new yarn in your project can be trouble-
some sometimes. Part of the problem is that there
are so many options to use and some work better
in different circumstances. There are different joins
depending on whether you are adding in a new
colour, an extra colour or adding in a new ball when
you've run out. There is an element of personal
preference too. I'm not a big fan of the Russian join,
but there are knitters that are. The best option is
to try them out for yourself and see which works
best for you.

First things first: please don't leave knots in your
knitting, especially if you want a good finish. They
can pop through to the front, you can feel them in
the fabric, they can potentially come undone and
there are so many other options for a better finish.
If your project has seams, then try and place the
joins where these seams will be as it's much easier to
invisibly darn the ends into seams rather than into
the fabric itself. However, there are a lot of projects
where there are no seams. If you have a shawl, then
it's tidier to make the joins in the fabric instead of
at the edge.

Open lace fabrics can be tricky to join in yarn.
Try and place the joins at any point in the pattern
where there are fewer eyelets, such as where there
might be a few knit stitches next to each other
rather than at a yarnover point.

Just start knitting

The downside to this is there is nothing restraining
the start and end stitch and they will likely look
loose as you work. This can be easily sorted
with the darning later, but if you're anything like
me, then you might find this untidiness, as you
work, irritating.

You don't have to do anything fancy when joining in yarn.
You can just finish with the old colour and start knitting with
the new yarn.

This is a method that adds no bulk, and you can get a perfect
finish with some judicious darning of ends later.

Slip knot join

The slip knot join is a technique that I use regularly. I saw Lucy Neatby do this quickly in her *Intarsia Untangled* DVD (2008), but I've never been able to find a tutorial for it. The new yarn is attached to the old with a slip knot and then slid down against the fabric. When you finish, you can just pull on the end of the yarn to quickly undo the knot. This can be sewn in neatly. This stops the obvious untidiness of the loose stitch as you work, yet gives that non-bulky and neat finish with the ends. Sometimes, smooth and silky finish yarns don't work brilliantly with this technique and the slip knot may slide a little, but as you're undoing it anyway at the end, this isn't a huge problem.

The slip knot join only works when you've finished knitting with the previous yarn and starting either a new colour or a new ball of yarn.

STEP-BY-STEP: SLIP KNOT JOIN

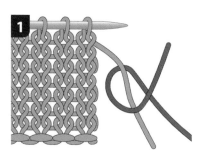

Step 1. Using new yarn, make a loop around the cut end of the old yarn.

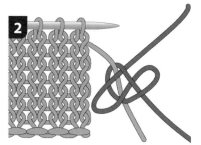

Step 2. Pull a loop of the end partially through the first loop created.

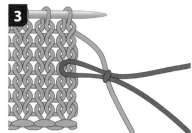

Step 3. Pull this loop and both ends firmly to create a slip knot around the old yarn.

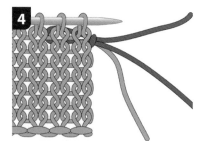

Step 4. Slide knot up the old yarn to fit tightly against the fabric.

Three-stitch join

This is another technique from Techknitter. Just work 3 stitches with both the new and old yarn. Later, when you have worked past this point, pull gently on both ends and this pulls the excess to the back and gives a neat finish. Don't trim the ends too close. This works very well with non-superwash yarns. If using slippery or superwash yarn, either work over 4 stitches or darn those ends in for extra insurance.

Weaving in as you go

This is a straightforward way of joining in the yarn and one I use regularly, though I'm never quite sold on the finish in some circumstances. In stocking stitch, this weaving in can be a little visible at times as there's a slight wave to the base of the stitches. It works far better in textured stitches, such as garter stitch.

The three-stitch join is simple and effective, but works best when using the same colour yarn, such as when joining in a new ball of the same colour.

Weaving in as you go involves trapping the yarn end above and below the working yarn as you knit.

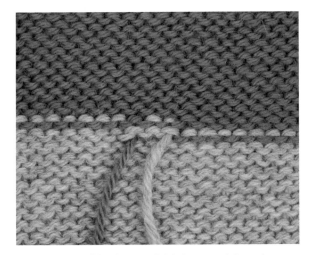

The wrong side of the three-stitch join is neat and the ends can just be trimmed to finish.

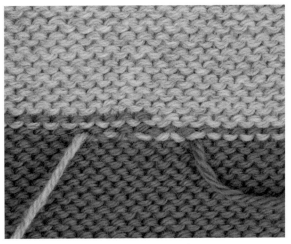

The wrong side of weaving as you go can be trimmed, though I prefer to weave in the opposite direction for extra security.

Often, I will just do this for 1 stitch to stop the yarn from moving as I work and then come back and darn this in later. If it's been woven over about 2.5cm (1in) then it should be fine to just cut the yarn, though fibres with a silkier finish may need to travel further. Personally, I prefer to have the certainty and will often use a darning needle to take the yarn back in the opposite direction before trimming the ends. This technique doesn't work brilliantly if some of the stitches are purled, as ideally, you need two consecutive stitches that are worked with the yarn at the back to trap the ends.

STEP-BY-STEP: WEAVING IN AS YOU GO

Step 1. You can trap the end of the new yarn by laying it over the needle with the end at the front and knitting the next stitch over this end.

Step 2. Insert the needle to knit the next stitch and hold the end to be woven in above the RHN. I find it easiest to hold the end in my left hand. Knit the stitch.

Step 3. On the following one, drop the old yarn down, knit the next stitch, so the working yarn traps it.

Step 4. Repeat for as many stitches as you want to weave the yarn across the back.

Clasp weft

In the clasp weft join, two ends are interlocked with each other and at least 6 stitches are worked across this doubled thread. The position of the join can be controlled, which is useful when changing colour. Work 3 stitches and mark the yarn at this point (either by holding it or placing a stitch marker through the yarn), undo the 3 stitches and make sure the join sits at this point. As you become more practised, this step won't be necessary and you'll be able to judge where to connect the loops.

Work with this doubled yarn until at least 3 stitches have been worked with the new yarn; then just continue in a single strand of the new yarn. The ends can be trimmed afterwards but not too close to the fabric, otherwise, the ends can pop to the front.

The clasp weft join is easy to work and secure, though there is a little extra bulk for a few stitches.

STEP-BY-STEP: CLASP WEFT JOIN

1

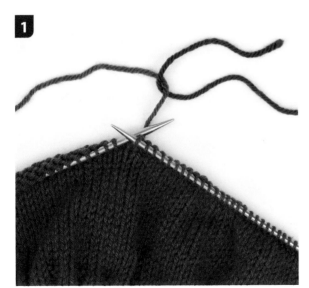

Step 1. Holding the old yarn to the left, take the new yarn and loop this over the strand.

2

Step 2. Hold both ends of the new yarn together and hold the old yarn with a little tension against the left-hand needle if you can. This will interlock the yarns.

Felted join

This is a fabulous yarn-saving and easy join but it has limited uses as it will only work with certain fibres. The fibre needs to be able to felt. Generally, it needs to be an animal fibre that hasn't been treated to be washable. A good first check to see if the yarn will felt is to see if the washing instructions say hand wash; if they do, then there's a good chance you can felt it. If in doubt, just give the technique a try and see if the join works.

Moisture and friction are the two components needed to felt fibres. The felted join has the other unpleasant name of 'spit splice' for good reasons. It's often easier than travelling to the nearest tap to get water, to instead use saliva to provide the moisture.

If the yarn is a single ply, then remove a little bit of fibre. Try to do this by pulling rather than using scissors as the frayed, feathered ends created by snapping the yarn give more surface for the felting to adhere to and will give a stronger join.

Ideally, the felted join wants to be used when joining in a new ball of the same colour.

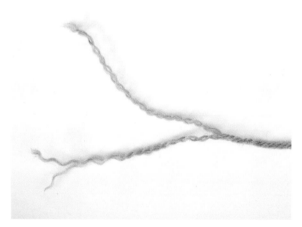

To make a smoother and stronger finish, remove a ply or two from each end to keep the width of the yarn the same at the join.

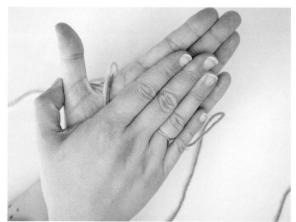

The basics behind the technique are to wet the yarn, overlap both ends and rub them together between your hands to create friction.

Magic knot

A word of caution with this one. I am not a fan. I will avoid a knot in my work. Even if you've placed it carefully, they have a tendency to move and be seen at the front of the work. Once you've made your knot give it a very vigorous tug to make sure it holds. It's not much fun to try and fix one that unravels at a later date.

My recommendation is to consider using this with scrappy projects only, where the changes of colour can hide the knots and to avoid using it with smooth fabrics, such as stocking stitch.

The magic knot is a clever little knot that reduces yarn wastage, is quick to work and is strong.

Step 1. Using each end, make an overhand knot with each over the other end.

Step 2. Pull tight.

Step 3. Slide to meet each other and trim ends.

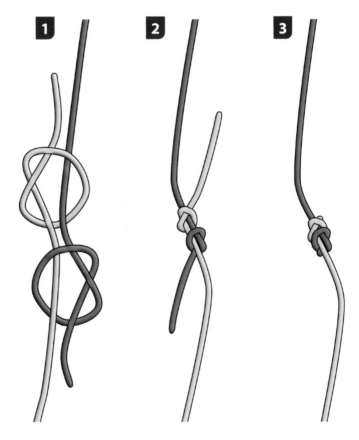

Russian join

The Russian join is another clever technique but not one I use very often. As well as being time consuming, the yarn is thicker at the join than elsewhere, so has more potential to be visible.

The Russian join is not the quickest join to create, but it is strong.

STEP-BY-STEP: RUSSIAN JOIN

Step 1. To create a Russian join, loop both ends together.

Step 2. Using a darning needle, catch the strand of the same loop for about 2.5–5cm (1–2in), and pull the needle through.

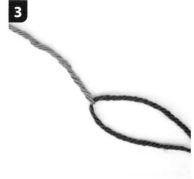

Step 3. Rethread the other end and repeat for the other loop.

Step 4. Pull and smooth out both loops and trim the ends.

To avoid that purl blip every time you change colour, work the first row/round of the new colour as a plain knit row. On the following rows, continue in the ribbing pattern. You would think this would interrupt the ribbing pattern, but that knit row recedes to the back of the work, making it hard to spot.

When working stripes in ribbing, you might have noticed that when you change colour, there are little blips of both colours in the purl columns. This stops a nice clean line at the joins.

This remarkably simple technique cleans up those lines.

STRIPES

Working stripes flat

There are a few situations where striping yarns can cause issues with untidiness. Most of the time when working flat with stripes, there's not any problem unless the edges are left visible, such as with a shawl or scarf. There are a couple of techniques to improve those edges. The first principle stems back to Chapter 1 and consistency. Whatever method you decide to use, stick with it. It will look correct.

When striping at the edges, try to take the new colour over the old one in the same manner each time. I always take my new colour over the top of the old one; that way, the wraps that are visible at the edge all look the same. However, there is a way to hide this colour wrapping.

Slipped stitches

Not every pattern will work for this, but it's useful if you can substitute this into your pattern. It's a technique that I include in my patterns if I can. Don't Fret and Variegata use this technique to hide the yarn wraps at the edge.

When changing colour at the edge, end the wrong side row with a slip stitch with the yarn held at the front. This means that when you come back to that yarn at the next colour change, it is sitting 1 stitch in from the edge and the wraps will be behind the work instead of at the edge.

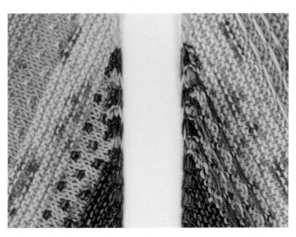

Left to right – front and reverse. The yarn wraps are not visible from the front and are hidden 1 stitch in on the wrong side.

Working stripes in the round

There's a unique problem when working stripes in the round – the jog. For neat stripes, the rings of colour want to be stacked on top of each other. However, when working in the round, you are continuously working in a spiral. This means that if you change colour at the start of the round, then one stitch will be a different colour to the one next to it. This will make both stripes look like there is a jog between the two.

The relevant factor is the number of rows in a stripe. If the stripes are single rows then helical knitting is the best option for a smooth finish. Any other depth of stripe, then jogless stripes are the easier option.

Stripes in the round will create a jog at the beginning of the round.

Jogless stripes – stretched stitch method

There are two different methods to get a similar result.

Both methods stretch a stitch to smooth the join; the first stretches the new colour and the second the old one. As the results are so similar, I tend to use the first method as it is a little quicker to work. The downside for both is that in this initial column, there will be one less row.

The first method is to slip the first stitch of the new colour when you come to it on the second row.

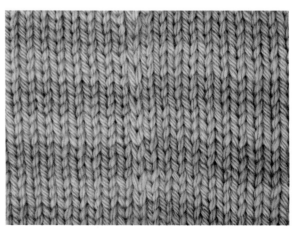

The second method is to work a round in the new colour, then at the beginning of the second round, pick up the stitch below the one with the new colour and knit this together with the new colour.

Jogless stripes – yarnover method

This works because the yarnover pushes the last stitch down and smooths out the jog. This can be worked for both single and continuous stripes. The yarn can remain attached when working multiple stripes and the yarnover is worked in the new colour in the same way, but the yarn is attached to the stripe below instead.

The yarnover method maintains the same number of stitches in every column.

When you need to join in the new colour, finish the previous round and then slip the last stitch back to the LHN, join the new colour by holding the end and then work a yarnover, slip the last stitch back to the RHN and continue in your new colour.

After working your first round, when you reach the yarnover and the last stitch of the round, knit these together. Continue working the remainder of the stripe in the new colour.

YARN MANAGEMENT WITH STRIPES IN THE ROUND

For stripes of two or more rows, when changing colour at the beginning of the round, take the old colour over the new one, so the two yarns are wrapped around each other. If you don't do this, then there will be a small hole at the colour change.

When swapping colours, make sure that you check the last stitch worked of the colour that you're about to start working with and make sure it hasn't been pulled up tight. Try to eyeball the tension on this stitch to match the surrounding stitches.

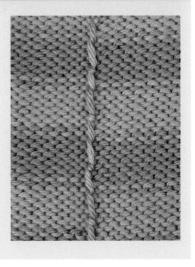

If you are working very deep striping, then it can help to rotate the unused yarn over the working one about every 4 rows to keep the strand connected to the fabric and this does help improve the tension at the yarn swap too.

Helical stripes

Helical stripes take advantage of the spiral construction when working in the round. Helical stripes are easy to work but can become a little confusing when trying to work them into a pattern, since you can't count your rounds in the same way as normal. The basic principle of helical knitting is to have a separate ball of yarn for every row of striping. This means that if you were to work 2 rows of your main colour and 1 row of your contrast, then you would need two balls of main colour and one ball of your contrast colour.

In the Dapper Spruce pattern (see Chapter 9: Projects), the 1-row striping is worked using this method. The stripes are 1-row stripes of two different colours, so one ball of each colour is needed.

Technically, helical knitting can be done by just swapping the yarn at the beginning of the round (as with normal striping) but don't twist the yarns over each other as you would with wider stripes. However, this can cause issues with tension. When changing from one colour to another, care should be taken not to pull the new colour too tight as the previous stitches in this yarn will not be sitting on a needle. This means that it is quite easy to close those stitches tight and cause uneven tension in the fabric that can be quite noticeable. To prevent this problem, there's an easy technique to fix this.

Work in one yarn until you are 3 stitches away from where you left the previous colour. Slip the 3 stitches purlwise and change to your new colour. This slipping of stitches stops you from pulling these stitches too tight as they remain sitting on the needle. The reason why it is 3 stitches, rather than another number, is that this is the minimum needed to maintain tension. If you had 2, then it's still possible to pull the yarn too tight. This does mean that you can slip more stitches or fewer, if you do it with care.

Often, the designer will place the start of the round in the least obvious place, so if in doubt, start and finish yarns there.

Left to right – front and reverse. One-row stripes in the round create a jog on the front, as well as a ridge of wraps on the wrong side.

Work in one colour until you are 3 stitches away from where you left the previous colour.

The start and end of a yarn in helical knitting can be visible, so try and place this where it isn't obvious to see, for example, a side seam, at the back or sole of a sock.

Tips and tricks for helical knitting

Working with a pattern or shaping in helical knitting can be a little tricky to visualize and keep track of. Try these tricks to make helical knitting easier.

- Use stitch markers in the fabric to mark rows worked. You can't count them as completed whenever you reach the beginning of the round, as you may not have worked a complete round of the other yarn.
- Upon reaching a section where there is a stitch pattern, you can always finish with one yarn just before this section and instead of just slipping 3 before the next yarn, slip all the stitches until you reach your second yarn. This means that the helical swap section will be before the pattern, and you can concentrate on the pattern and not be concerned about having a swap partway through.
- The same principle works with shaping. If the pattern allows, move the helical swap to before the shaping.
- Eventually, the helical swap may move back into a patterned or shaped section. Just move the helical swap point again.
- Sometimes, this isn't possible and the helical swap might be in the middle of a decrease. For example, you need to work a k2tog just before a helical swap but there are 4 stitches left and 2 are needed for the k2tog and that would only leave 2 stitches to slip. That isn't a problem; simply work the k2tog and just slip 2 stitches instead.

EXAMPLE OF CONVERTING A PATTERN TO HELICAL KNITTING

In Dapper Spruce, the instructions for the single row stripes read as follows:

- **Round 1:** using CC2, knit.
- **Round 2:** using CC1, knit.

To change this, work Round 1 until 3 stitches from the end of the round. Slip the last 3 stitches purlwise. Change to CC1 and work Round 2 until 3 stitches before where CC2 has been left.

*Slip the next 3 stitches purlwise and change to CC2. Knit until 3 sts before CC1, slip the next 3 stitches purlwise. Change to CC1, knit until 3 sts before CC2. Continue in this manner, repeating from *. To get that perfect finish when at the desired length, finish with the first colour at the beginning of the round and slip all the stitches until you reach the second colour and knit to the end of the round. Both yarns will have started and finished at the beginning of the round.

CHAPTER 5

EDGES

GRAFTING

Grafting, also known as Kitchener stitch, is one of those techniques that knitters will often avoid; perhaps, it's the fact that you're sewing instead of knitting. It can be an especially useful technique to have in your toolkit though. We'll talk about sewn seams in Chapter 7, but they can have issues with untidiness and they will be tighter than the knitted fabric. Using grafting instead gives the same result – two edges joined together – but it replicates a knitted row with the same stretch as the rest of the knitting. This means that it can be the better choice for a professional finish in some circumstances, such as sock toes, folded hems and the like.

The first factor to consider is whether you are grafting the top and bottom of the fabric – or top and top together. This is all about the direction of the knitting. For example, in Dapper Spruce (see Chapter 9: Projects), you are grafting top and bottom stitches together as you are joining the cast-on and final rows together. However, if you were joining a traditional sock toe, then this would be joining top and top stitches, as both sets of stitches would be where you've finished knitting.

Top-to-bottom grafting

This is the method used in Dapper Spruce. Normally, you will know that you want to do this in advance and the piece will have a provisional cast-on, so it is easy to undo the edge to put the live stitches on the needle. Occasionally, you might want to place stitches on a needle because you want to alter the length and haven't planned in advance. Use the reactive lifeline method in this situation – see Chapter 8.

How to graft

When grafting top to bottom, you will be creating a full line of knitting with a darning needle. The traditional way of grafting is to have the stitches on the knitting needles. When worked on the needles, half the stitches are on each needle. The needles are held parallel with the tips pointing to the right. The yarn needs to be cut to four times the width of the seam that will be grafted. Often, this yarn will be attached to the final stitch of the knitting, but a separate piece can be used too. Just leave a long enough end to darn in afterwards. Thread the yarn on to a darning needle.

It's a lot more of a manageable process if you work the following steps in pairs. It's more efficient as you are pulling the yarn through half as much, and if you get interrupted partway through then it's easier to figure out what step you've reached.

When it is time to put those stitches back onto the needles, there are two options to choose from.

One factor to bear in mind is you are not picking up a full stitch from a provisional edge, instead you are picking up the loops between the needles. This means that there will be one less full stitch to pick up than stitches cast on. The remaining stitch is made up of half a stitch at either side.

However, if you are working in a stitch pattern that remains the same across the row, such as stocking stitch, it will not be obvious if you use the half loop as a full stitch. However, if the pattern changes, such as ribbing, it is important to maintain those half loops, as the grafting will not line up correctly. Since you are working into the down bar of the stitch, then if knitting from this direction, just bear in mind that all the stitches will be offset by half a stitch. Try and make sure there is a change in stitch pattern, so that this is not obvious.

Find where the crochet chain finished and start to unravel the chain and place each stitch onto the needle as you go.

Alternatively, pick up the right-hand leg of every stitch under the chain first and then undo the provisional cast-on afterwards.

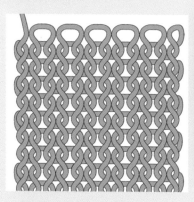

At the side opposite the tail, there is a small loop, which is one half of a stitch and the other can be created by looping the tail over the needle.

As you can see in this 1 × 1 ribbing, the jog at the provisional join is obvious.

Setup Step 1. Insert the needle purlwise into the stitch on the front needle and pull through.

Setup Step 2. Insert the needle knitwise into the stitch on the back needle and pull through.

For example, if the yarn is coming from a stitch on the front needle, you need to continue from Step 2 and vice versa, if the yarn is coming from the back needle, continue from Step 1.

Tension is important with grafting. When you pull the yarn through each stitch, try and make them the same size as the rest of the stitches. If at the end some of the stitches are different sizes, you can use a needle tip to resize them and if there's any excess yarn produced, then move this to where the grafting finished.

Step 1a. Insert the needle knitwise into the stitch on the front needle and remove from the knitting needle (use the darning needle to lift the stitch off). Don't pull the yarn through yet.

Step 1b. Insert the needle purlwise into the stitch on the front needle and pull through.

Step 2a. Insert the needle purlwise into the stitch on the back needle and remove from the knitting needle. Don't pull the yarn through yet.

Step 2b. Insert the needle knitwise into the stitch on the back needle and pull through. Repeat Steps 1 and 2 until all stitches have been worked.

The grafted row should look like the rest of rows. The grafted row is the top magenta row on the central stripe.

Top-to-top grafting

Top-to-top grafting is different because you're joining the tops of two sets of stitches together. This means that the graft will be offset by half a stitch. Try to use top-to-top grafting where the same stitch is worked across the entire row to make the jog less obvious. The most common situation to do this type of grafting is in a sock toe.

Since the stitches are offset slightly, this can lead to 'ears' of fabric at the corners of the sock toes, due to the offset half stitches. The easiest way to avoid these ears is to skip the half-stitch setup on the first 2 stitches, that is, start at Step 1 instead of the 'setup' steps. When 2 stitches are left on each needle, complete Steps 1 and 2 as normal but remove all the stitches from the knitting needles.

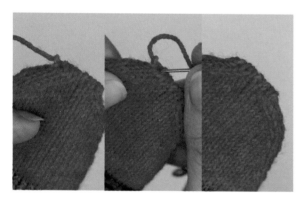

The last stitch will look a bit large and loose. Just take the needle through to the wrong side directly behind this loop, so it is pulled to the reverse.

Garter stitch grafting

Garter stitch grafting is an easier process than for stocking stitch, as the same steps are repeated on each needle. However, you do need to make sure you have finished at the right point in your knitting, so the grafted row is at the correct place to continue the garter stitch.

- **Setup step 1:** Insert the needle purlwise into the stitch on the front needle and pull through.
- **Setup step 2:** Insert the needle purlwise into the stitch on the back needle and pull through.
- **Step 1a:** Insert the needle knitwise into the stitch on the front needle and remove from the knitting needle (use the darning needle to lift the stitch off). Don't pull the yarn through yet.
- **Step 1b:** Insert the needle purlwise into the next stitch on the front needle and pull through.
- **Step 2a:** Rep Step 1a on the back needle.
- **Step 2b:** Rep Step 1b on the back needle.
- Rep Steps 1 and 2 until all the stitches have been worked.

When grafting in garter stitch, each needle should have the purl bumps from the previous row next to the needle on the side of the knitting facing you.

PICKING UP STITCHES

Picking up stitches is used when you need to work from an edge of your knitting. The most common uses are for button bands and necklines, though it can be used as part of the construction too, as in the Deft pattern (see Chapter 9: Projects). There is a slight difference between instructions to 'pick up' and to 'pick up and knit'. Most instructions will be 'pick up and knit', but occasionally, you'll just pick up part of the edge and place on the needle without knitting. The 'pick up and knit' gives a much neater finish, as the edge stitches are not stretched out on a needle, so if you have the option, use this technique.

Many patterns will tell you to 'pick up and knit' a specific number of stitches, for example, 160 stitches along a button band. This can be tricky to get right. It's common to find yourself at the end and need to pick up more stitches or have too many. It's frustrating to have to pull the work back to try again. Stitch markers can make this process easier.

Using stitch markers to help pick up exact numbers

For example, there are 160 stitches to pick up down the side of a button band. Break the side into smaller sections. Fold the edge in half and place a marker. Fold each section in half again and place more markers. This can be done as often or as little as needed.

If you find yourself having to pick up a specific number of stitches, stitch markers can be helpful.

Divide the stitch count by the number of sections, for example, 160/4 = 40 stitches.

By having smaller sections, you can get the stitches spread evenly and if your count is incorrect, it's a smaller number to take back. Once a section is correct, move the marker onto the needle and work the next section. This saves a lot of frustration.

Ratio of picking up

Even if the pattern tells you to pick up a specific number of stitches, you don't necessarily have to follow it. The pattern is relying on you getting your stitch count and row count to match the recommended gauge. In my experience, it's very difficult to match both exactly. If your row gauge is incorrect, then you could pick up too many stitches and get a wavy edge, or too few and make the main body ruffle instead.

Many bands and edges tend to be simple stitch patterns such as ribbing or garter stitch. It all depends on the stitch multiples on how much you can adjust the edging. 1 × 1 ribbing has a stitch multiple of 2, so you can adjust the number by this, that is, you can add or subtract sets of 2 from the stitch count. However, if the stitch multiple is quite large, then altering the stitch numbers might not be the best option and a change in needle size would be easier than altering the pattern.

The number of stitches picked up is determined by the ratio of the stitches to the rows. An example gauge of 22 stitches by 30 rows would have an approximate ratio of 3 stitches to 4 rows. Therefore, if you were using the same needle for the band, you would pick up 3 stitches in adjacent rows and then skip 1 row. However, many patterns will use a smaller needle for the bands, so this ratio will be different. For example, the main pattern has been worked using 4mm [US size 6] and the band will use 3.25mm [US size 3]. The gauge on 3.25mm will be 27 stitches by 36 rows. The ratio of the 3.25mm stitches to the 4mm rows is approximately 7 stitches to 8 rows.

I'm going to explain working out your ratio for yourself to get perfect edges but if in doubt, use 3 stitches to 4 rows when using the same needle and when using a needle 2 to 3 sizes smaller, use 7 stitches to 8 rows.

Working out your exact pickup ratio

If you've done a swatch beforehand, you will know the gauge of the main body of work. However, if for whatever reason you haven't, then it's easy to find those numbers. Steam or spray block a section of your work and measure that. For this example, let's use 22 stitches by 30 rows.

If you're using a different needle size, then you need the stitch gauge for that needle too. You might be lucky and have used the stitch pattern elsewhere in the project – just use this as your swatch. If not, then work a swatch in the stitch pattern that's going to be used. You don't need to make it as long as normal, since you don't need the row gauge number. Block to get your stitch gauge. If it's ribbing, then you can gently stretch it to how you want it to look before measuring. Let's say this gauge is 27 stitches by 36 rows.

To work out the ratio, divide the stitches of the edge gauge by the rows of the main needle, for example, 27/30 = 0.9. That number isn't very helpful on its own. To assist, Table 1 outlines some common ratios; just pick the one that is nearest to your number. In this example, 7 stitches in 8 rows would be the best ratio when using the 3.25mm needle. If you are using the same size needle, then it would by 22/30 = 0.73. The nearest ratio is 0.75, so pick up 3 stitches in 4 rows instead.

You can make these numbers more exact. For example, I could round 22 stitches and 30 rows down to their smallest whole numbers, for example, 11 stitches in 15 rows and then work out how to

Table 1   Pickup ratios for different figures

Ratio number found from dividing stitches by rows	Pickup ratio
0.50	1 stitch in 2 rows
0.60	3 stitches in 5 rows
0.66	2 stitches in 3 rows
0.75	3 stitches in 4 rows
0.80	4 stitches in 5 rows
0.85	6 stitches in 7 rows
0.90	7 stitches in 8 rows
1.00	1 stitch in 1 row

spread that evenly, so there are no adjacent skipped stitches. The exact pick up would be pick up 2, skip 1, (pick up 3, skip 1) three times. However, knitting is quite forgiving, so rounding to the numbers in the table will give you a straight edge without any complex maths.

Garter stitch

When the main fabric is worked in garter stitch, or any other fabric that has more compressed rows than stocking stitch, such as stranded or slipped stitches, then the ratios will be different. Since there are more rows in garter stitch, then picking up 1 stitch in 2 rows is a better ratio.

Picking up stitches along the side edge

As I mentioned in Chapter 1, consistency is key here. The traditional place to pick up on a side edge is a full stitch in. However, whichever column you use, make sure that it remains the same along the entire length. It is often this column movement that makes picking up look untidy.

If you keep the pick-up consistent, then you'll get a beautiful straight line from the main fabric.

Treat the knitted edge like your left-hand needle. Insert the RHN into a stitch from front to back and to check you're in the edge stitch, look how many strands are on your needle – there should be 2.

Take the yarn around the needle as if to knit and, keeping tension on the yarn, pull back through to the front. Re-insert the RHN into the next stitch up – there should just be one vertical bar in between then repeat.

If you have no edge treatment on the piece, then the edge stitch tends to roll around and sit at the back of the work. Ensure that you are working into this stitch – tilt the knitting towards you, so you can see the back of the fabric as you work. The actual picking up can be done with one needle, two needles or even a crochet hook. My preference is the one-needle method, as it is relatively quick and there's only one needle opening the stitches, so it doesn't over-stretch them. To give smooth edges, start your pickup directly into the cast on/off row.

If you are skipping stitches, try to do this on the smaller stitches, if possible. When skipping stitches, there should be two vertical bars in between. Don't skip two adjacent stitches. For example, if you need to work 3 stitches in 5 rows, work this as pick up 2, skip 1, pick 1, skip 1. If you struggle to pull the yarn through, then the two-needle or crochet method might help. The two-needle method involves inserting the LHN into the stitch and then using the RHN to knit this as normal. Alternatively, a crochet hook is inserted instead of the needle and the yarn scooped through and then placed on the knitting needle.

Picking up stitches along the top

Necklines and collars are often picked up from a combination of side and top edges. For top edges, you are picking up into stitches instead of rows, so the ratio will be different. If the same needle size is used, then pick up into every stitch. Technically, if a smaller needle is used, then you'll likely want to pick up more stitches. However, most of the time, this is done for necklines, and you don't want a perfectly straight edge as it curves into the neck, so the numbers will be fewer. It is best to use the numbers in the pattern for necklines, as there are other factors in play.

Picking up stitches along a curve

A curved edge is often created with a combination of shaped vertical edges and cast-off sections. There is something that can be done to make picking up stitches far easier when there is shaping. As mentioned in Chapter 3, ensure that you don't work any increases or decreases in the edge stitch. If you work them 1 or 2 stitches in, then you have a single clean column all the way up the piece and it makes it far easier to maintain a neat finish.

With any picking up that isn't into a clean edge, then regularly look at it as you work. If there is anything that is showing a hole or is not as neat as you like, redo it.

When the edge is shaped and it changes from cast off to decreasing/increasing, then there's often a small hole. Don't be tempted to pick up into the hole, as this just makes it bigger. Skip to the next space instead and this will close the hole. Just keep checking though, and if that hasn't worked as you'd like, try a different space instead.

The principle is the same whether picking up from a cast-on or cast-off edge, though picking up from the cast-off edge is far more common.

To get a perfect column of stitches, insert the needle tip into the centre of the V to pick up the stitches. The picked-up stitch, once worked, will look as if the knit column has continued perfectly.

Use a combination of the picking up from the side on the vertical parts and into the centre of the stitches on the cast-off sections for a curved edge.

Picking up stitches at a V-neck

V-necks are easier to work than curved necklines, as the edges are shaped side edges, so you can be consistent along the edge. However, I always err on the side of extra stitches for an angled edge, since it tends to be a little longer than a fully vertical edge. If you've kept your shaping out of the edge stitch, then it will be easy to pick up.

When shaping the V-neck, you can keep the central stitch on a marker then the knitting can run smoothly into the centre of the V. If you're using pairs of decreases then it won't be centralized, so no need to do that.

When working a V-neck, it gives a very neat finish if the decreases at the centre of the V are worked as centred double decreases.

PICKING UP ACROSS CORNERS

There are some situations where it can be easy to create holes when picking up stitches. The most common areas for this are when there is 3D shaping such as armholes, thumbs, heels and so on. If you pick up as normal at either side, the likelihood of a hole is high. Instead, try and close the hole with the picking up by working a stitch into part of a stitch on either side of the gap. Always check this before continuing and if you aren't happy with the finish, try a different spot to close any gaps.

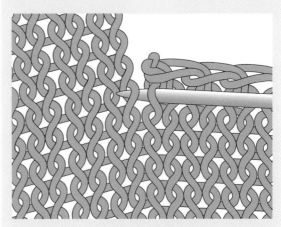

To close the gap, pick up the left leg of the right-hand stitch and the right leg of the left-hand stitch.

Converting sewn-on edges

Some patterns will have a band that is worked in a long strip and then sewn into place. There's nothing wrong with this but it's easy to knit it too long or short, or sew it on too tightly. It's far easier to change the instructions to convert this to a pickup instead.

Using a separate piece of yarn (or measure out four times the width and work towards the end of the yarn), pick up and knit along the edge where the pattern instructs you to attach the band. The pickup ratio will be different to a normal band, as you will be working 2 rows of the band for every pickup stitch.

You need the row gauge of the main fabric and the row gauge of your band. Divide the band gauge by two and then use the pickup ratio instructions earlier in the chapter to work out how many stitches. For example, the row gauge for the main fabric is 30 and 36 for the band. Divide 36 in half, so 18 rows.

18/30 = 0.6 ratio. The nearest figure on the chart is 3 stitches in 5 rows. In practical terms, this will be pick up 2 sts, skip 1, pick up 1 st, skip 1.

On another needle, work the band as instructed but at the end of every RS row, work the final stitch as an SSK with one of the picked-up stitches on the other needle. On the WS, slip this stitch and work the rest of the band as instructed.

This gives a beautiful flat edge with no sewing.

SELVEDGES

The edges of your project can be a key factor in the finish of the piece. If you have a wavy or untidy edge, that is the first thing that catches the eye. If your project is seamed together, the edges won't be visible and the finish of those edges is less important. However, if they are on full display, such as in a scarf or shawl, then to get that professional finish, it's important to get those edges looking tidy.

Seamed selvedges

When the edge is going to be hidden in the seam, often the best technique to use is to work those edges in stocking stitch. If you happen to struggle finding the correct place to sew up, you can work a single stitch at the edge in garter stitch. My preference is stocking stitch, as you don't have to remember to treat the edge stitch differently.

There's a temptation to use a slipped stitch edge when seaming, but it doesn't help for two reasons. Firstly, it prevents you from easing in the edge as you only have 1 stitch for every 2 rows and secondly, if you use a slipped stitch, there is a small gap created next to this stitch. This isn't noticeable in a shawl but if you seam this edge instead, the seam pulls on these small gaps making them bigger.

Visible selvedges

Stocking stitch is not a great choice for a selvedge since all the stitches are going in the same direction, and it tends to roll inwards. This distorts the edge and hides the stitch pattern. There are lots of alternatives that give a flatter finish. Most of them are decorative and can often be substituted for each other.

Garter stitch selvedge

One of the main features of garter stitch is that it lies flat. This makes it a perfect pairing for edges as it stops the edge rolling inwards. Another alternative is when a garter stitch edge is combined with a

Any number of stitches can be worked in garter stitch, though for a true selvedge this will normally be one to three stitches.

Left to right – Moss stitch (also known as seed stitch) and ribbing are two good alternatives for selvedges.

chained selvedge. This gives the side seam a nice smooth finish, but with the benefit of the garter stitch to keep it from rolling.

Other stitch patterns

Any combination of knit and purl can be used as a selvedge. As long as all the stitches are not all the same, then it shouldn't roll. The purl stitches in a ribbed selvedge recede to the back of the fabric. This means that at a distance you can be fooled to think it is stocking stitch, which can be a helpful technique.

I-cord and double selvedges

Another favourite of designers is to use i-cord as an edging. The i-cord creates a thick vertical line at the edge and when combined with garter stitch, this creates a beautiful juxtaposition of angles. It does work better when used with garter stitch, as only 1 row is worked for 2 of the fabric and in stocking stitch, this will distort over a large piece of fabric.

* **RS:** ...wyif sl 3.
* **WS:** k3...

The double stocking stitch selvedge is a good alternative to an i-cord. It has a slightly different construction for a similar result.

* **RS:** k1, wyif sl 1 pw, k1, ..., k1, wyif sl 1 pw, k1.
* **WS:** wyif sl 1 pw, p1, wyif sl 1 pw, ..., wyif sl 1 pw, p1, wyif sl 1 pw.

Chained selvedges

A chained selvedge is a stitch at the edge that has been slipped, so that it travels over 2 rows. This creates a 'chain' at the edge.

The *English* method is worked as follows:
* **RS:** sl 1 kw,... , sl 1 kw.
* **WS:** p1,... , p1.

The *French* method is worked as follows:
* **RS:** sl 1 kw,... , k1.
* **WS:** sl 1 pw,... , p1.

If using this method for garter stitch, then on the WS, take the yarn back between the needles after slipping the first stitch.

The *German* method is worked as follows:
If working stocking stitch:
* **RS:** k1,... , wyib sl 1 pw.
* **WS:** p1,... , wyif sl 1 pw.

Left to right – I-cord and double stocking stitch selvedges both create a rounded edge.

Top to bottom: German, English and French chained selvedge. The chained selvedge can be created in multiple different ways, but the results tend to be similar, if not identical.

If working garter stitch:
* **Both sides:** k1,... , wyif sl 1 pw.

The English and French methods create identical slipped stitches on each side. However, the German method creates mirrored stitches. Though if you want to make them matching in stocking stitch, swap the RS row for k1,... , wyib sl 1 kw.

My preference is the German method, as I mentioned in Chapter 4, since it allows the colour change to sit 1 stitch in. This means that if using more than one colour, the yarn swap is hidden from the front of the work.

FLIPPING HEMS

Many patterns will have a different stitch pattern at the bottom edge to stop the fabric from curling. The most common will be either garter stitch or ribbing. However, if nothing is done to compensate for the change in stitch, these hems will flip up. There is one technique to try after the knitting. Blocking will have some impact on the look of the flipping hem, especially if you've used natural fibres (see Chapter 7).

However, here are several more effective techniques to apply that will reduce this flip, though they all need to be done as you create the band and not after the fact.

- Use a needle two to three sizes smaller than the main needle.
- Reduce the number of stitches in the band by 10 per cent and increase them back when moving to the main fabric. For example, the instructions are to cast on 100 stitches. Cast on 10 per cent fewer, that is, 90 stitches. When the band has been completed, work an increase row where these 10 stitches are spread evenly across the row, for example, k4, m1, (k9, m1) nine times, k5.
- Work a deeper welt. This is not the most ideal solution on its own, but works well when paired with other techniques. Having more rows to weigh down the edge before the change in tension will help it to lie flatter. I would suggest a minimum of 2.5cm (1in); thinner edges than this are more likely to flip.
- If working in ribbing, when changing to the body fabric, work 1 row where all the knit stitches have been slipped purlwise with the yarn in the back, and work the purl stitches as normal.

Flipping hems can be caused by a combination of the change in stitch energy and difference in gauge.

Top to bottom: smaller needle, reduced number of stitches and original flip with no technique.

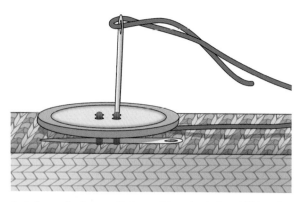

Just place a darning needle (or anything of a similar width) on the top of the fabric and then the button on top. Sew the button on with this is place.

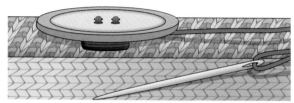

Finish with the thread at the front of the fabric but under the button. Once it's secure then remove the darning needle and wrap around the vertical threads under the button to create a thread shank and then take the thread to the back to secure.

BUTTONS

There are two main types of buttons – those with shanks and those with holes. The shank is there to allow the button to lie flat when closed and stop any distortion of the fabric. If you have a button with holes, you can create a thread shank easily as you attach the button.

One key factor to sewing on buttons is to position them in the correct place. It's surprisingly easy to misalign them. Use stitch markers to mark the correct position. Lay the garment flat and pin the marker to the button band through the button-hole and you'll get perfect positioning. When sewing them, it's best practice to use the same fibre content in the thread and the fabric. Ideally, this means that the yarn is the perfect choice for sewing the button. However, it is often too large to go through the holes on the button and splitting the plies will weaken the yarn too much to keep the button secure. Therefore,

sewing thread is the easier option. I like to use cotton over polyester, as it is less likely to cut through the fabric.

Sometimes, you'll get distortion at the button bands if the buttons are too heavy, or the fabric doesn't have much structure. You can sew ribbon to the back of the button band to reinforce it, or use a backing button or piece of felt at the wrong side of the fabric to reinforce where the button is attached.

BUTTONHOLES

One-row buttonholes

There are many ways to make buttonholes. The most common is casting off stitches on 1 row and casting them back on the subsequent row. This can be untidy and create small holes. Substituting these for one-row buttonholes gives a neater finish.

STEP-BY-STEP: ONE-ROW BUTTONHOLE

Work out how many stitches you need for your button. Place your button on your edge fabric and see how many stitches it covers. The buttonhole wants to be a little smaller than the button, so make it 1 stitch smaller; for example, if the button covers 6 stitches, the buttonhole will be 5 stitches wide.

Step 1. When you are at your buttonhole position, bring the yarn to the front between the needles. Slip the next stitch purlwise and then take the yarn to the back between the needles.

Step 2. *Slip the next stitch purlwise and then pass the previous stitch over this slipped stitch, repeat from * until one less buttonhole stitch is cast off. There are 4 stitches in our example. Slip the last stitch to LHN.

Step 3. Turn work. Cast on buttonhole stitches, for example, 5 stitches. Preferred method – cable cast-on purlwise for matching edges (see below).

Step 4. Turn to right side, slip next stitch purlwise and pass the last cast on stitch over. You've completed your one-row buttonhole.

CABLE CAST-ON PURLWISE

This cast-on gives the neatest finish when casting on for buttonholes. Using the cable cast-on purlwise creates a matching finish on the front, but it can be done knitwise too (just remember to bring the yarn to the front of the work before placing the last stitch on the LHN, otherwise the yarn will be on the incorrect side). To cable cast on purlwise, insert RHN from back to front between first 2 stitches on LHN and purl a stitch, then place this on the LHN.

Left to right. Cable cast-on knitwise and cable cast-on purlwise give a different look to the buttonhole.

Eyelet buttonholes

Another common buttonhole is an eyelet. This is quick and easy to create, but only works for small buttons. When worked in 1 × 1 ribbing, work the eyelet after a knit stitch, then yo, k2tog. In 2 × 2 ribbing, work the eyelet after a k2, then yo, p2tog.

Eyelet buttonholes are created by a yarnover and decrease placed next to each other.

CHAPTER 6

CASTING OFF

Arguably, casting off can be the most important of the edge stitches. In our projects, we
can come across untidy cast-offs or even
worse, the cast-off that is too tight. The tight cast-off
can turn a beautiful project into something unwear-
able. Maybe you can relate? It can be frustrating to
reach the end of a sweater and you've just cast off
for the neckline, only to find when you put it on
that it won't go over your head. I've been there too.
Luckily, you can always redo your cast-off, if you're
not happy with it. Plus, there are a variety of cast-
offs to try.

CASTING OFF IN THE MIDDLE OF THE ROW

Casting off in the middle of the row can involve
untidiness. Commonly, this technique is used when
casting off the neckline of a bottom-up sweater,
although there are other situations, such as pockets,
thumbholes and so on. There's a tendency to create
small holes at either side of this cast-off, which can
then be made to look worse with the picking up.
Thankfully, Techknitter has created a helpful technique for casting off in the middle of the row.

Start of casting off in the middle
Work to 1 stitch before the first cast-off stitch and
work kfb into that final stitch. Use the second half
of the kfb as the first stitch for the cast-off (but
don't include it in your count). Continue casting
off as normal.

Top: has no treatment. Bottom: uses the kfb to close the gap.

End of casting off in the middle
Continue to cast off until there are 2 stitches left
to cast off. Knit the first one, slip the next stitch
and pass the first knit stitch over the slipped stitch,
slip this stitch back to the LHN and k2tog with the
following stitch.

SLOPED CAST-OFFS

A traditional shoulder is not cast off in one straight
line; instead, it is a stepped cast off that creates an
angled edge allowing for the shape of a shoulder.
When sections are cast off on different rows like
this, it creates an uneven edge that can be difficult
and untidy to sew together.

There's an easy tip to change this stepped edge
into a smoother one, which makes it easier to sew
up. For example, say the pattern instructs you to cast
off 4 stitches at the beginning of every RS row until 5
stitches remain; cast off the first time as normal, but
when returning to the cast-off edge on the WS row,
finish 1 stitch earlier and slip this stitch purlwise
instead. Turn the work ready for the next 4-stitch
cast-off, slip the first 2 stitches purlwise (instead of
knitting them), and bind off the first stitch. Cast off
the remaining stitches as normal. Repeat this for
each cast-off section.

ALTERING SHOULDERS

A sewn shoulder can be beneficial to a good
construction of a garment. Most of the weight of a
garment hangs from the shoulders and a firm sewn
seam can give the garment strength and stop any
distortion. However, it can be difficult to get every
stitch to line up at the shoulder and give a neat
finish. Plus we're knitters – we want to knit, not
sew, right?

A cast-off and then sewn shoulder instruction
can be changed for a short-row shoulder and

Top: has no treatment. Bottom: uses the slip and k2tog technique.
The original technique is good when the edge is visible, as it is
still neat. The slip and k2tog technique keeps the column intact,
which gives a smoother finish when there is subsequent picking
up around this edge.

Top: a standard stepped cast-off edge. Bottom: using the
technique to create a sloped cast-off.

three-needle bind-off. This lends itself best to thinner yarns, as there is less weight hanging on the shoulders. Personally, I tend to avoid using this for yarns that are aran weight and thicker, but it's a personal choice. Should you find that you've used this technique and you're missing the stability of a sewn seam, then you can sew ribbon to the inside of the seam to stop it stretching. I've never found that I've needed to do that myself, but it gives you the option if you're unsure whether this will suit your garment.

The basic principle is to substitute the cast-off stitches for short rows. This means that where the end point of each cast-off section would be, that is, just before the final stitch cast off each time, you would knit to that point and work a short row instead. Work back to the neck edge and then knit to the next final cast-off point and repeat. I tend to use German short rows for doing this, as they're easy and invisible – see Chapter 3. Once all the short rows are worked, then work back across the row and work all the double stitches as one. The stitches are left live on a stitch holder or waste yarn. This is repeated for all the shoulder seams.

Once you have your short-row shaped shoulders, then you'll need a third needle. The RHN will be the one that determines the size of the cast-off, so ensure that's the size you need but the other two

EXAMPLE OF ALTERING A SHOULDER

The original pattern instructs us to cast off 4 stitches at the shoulder edge every other row until 5 stitches remain. There are 25 shoulder stitches, so there should be 5 short-row stitches worked when complete.

For the right shoulder, start on a RS row. For a left shoulder, start on a WS. Work to 5 stitches from the end, work a short row and turn; work to the end of the row. On the next row, work to 4 stitches before the previous short row, work a short row and turn; work to the end of the row. Repeat this until all the short rows have been worked. Work across the entire row working in any double short-row stitches as 1 stitch.

The easiest way in practice to work this out is to initially place a lockable stitch marker on your needle at every point where the cast-off would finish, for example, the first marker would go between stitches 4 and 5, the second marker between 8 and 9, and so on. This way you don't have to count and can just work a short row before each marker.

can be smaller, if you don't have two pairs of the same size. Place the front and back pieces of the same shoulder with right sides facing and the needle tips pointed to the right. This technique creates a visible line across the top, so ensure you have the right sides facing; otherwise, this will be visible on the outside.

Knit a stitch from the front needle and the back needle together, repeat and then cast off the first stitch. Repeat this until all stitches are cast off.

You should have a neat seam with all the stitches aligned together.

Should you find that the number of stitches on the front and back differ slightly, then you can decrease any extra stitches on the final row of the shoulder, or knit 1 stitch from one needle and 2 stitches from the other (that has the larger number) together.

CAST-OFF TOOLKIT

There are countless methods for casting off, also known as binding off. My cast-off toolkit has the methods that I use the most and I find to give the neatest finish, but is far from an exhaustive list. There are plenty of others to add to your own toolkit.

Traditional cast-off

The most common is the traditional or chain cast-off. It is the first one taught and for some people, the only one they will use. It is created by working a stitch and another, then the right-hand stitch is passed over the left-hand stitch and off the needle. The traditional cast-off can be worked in either knit or purl, or a combination of the two. If you have a ribbed edge, work the stitches as they appear and the cast-off will have a seamless finish.

This is an easy method but it can have a tendency to be tight and restrictive, which can easily ruin a project. There are a couple of different ways that this can be rectified. If you think about the practicalities, when working a cast-off stitch and passing it over the next, it not only has to travel its normal stitch height but across to the other side of the adjacent stitch. This is why the cast-off edge can be too tight. The solution is to make those stitches taller.

If you recall, in Chapter 1, I talked about the 'perfect' knit stitch, where you kept the needle tips together when removing the stitch from the needle. I'm going to suggest doing the exact opposite for casting off. Instead of keeping those needle tips together, pull the RHN towards the right immediately and this will give some extra height to those stitches – try to be consistent though. Ideally, there wants to be a bit of space under the stitches on the

Top: casting off in the same size needle. Bottom: casting off in a needle 2mm larger. The larger needle gives much more stretch and a less restrictive edge. However, they both look neat and similar in size.

In my pattern, Gentle Blooms, the cowl needed a stretchier edge, but I wanted to maintain the look of the chained edge. It was made using a 3.75mm (US Size 5) needle and the cast-off is worked with a 6.5mm (US Size 10.5) and the edge still looks consistent with the stitches.

RHN. This is the method that I use as it requires no other equipment. However, you might find it difficult to create consistent stitches with this method without practice. A good alternative is to use a larger needle for the cast-off instead. This makes all the stitches consistently larger. Have a try and don't worry about having the stitches too large; it's quite surprising how large you can make them, and it still looks consistent and neat.

Lori's twisty cast-off

Created by Loraine LeGrand, Lori's twisty cast-off works best with alternating knit and purl stitch edges, such as 1 × 1 ribbing, moss/seed stitch and so on. It can be worked for wider ribbing too. If starting with a knit stitch, knit the stitch, then start at Step 1; or if with a purl stitch, purl the stitch, then start at Step 2.

It is quite simple to adjust for different types of ribbing, for example, 2 × 2 ribbing and so on. If the next stitch is the same as the one as just worked, that is, knit stitch, followed by another knit stitch, just use the traditional cast-off as normal. If the next stitch is changing, then if it is changing to a purl, rotate anticlockwise and if it is a knit stitch, then rotate clockwise.

Lori's twisty cast-off gives a decorative, yet elastic edge.

STEP-BY-STEP: LORI'S TWISTY CAST-OFF

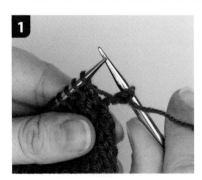

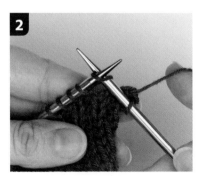

Step 1. Rotate RHN anticlockwise and back to centre. The yarn should have moved to the front of the work. Purl the next stitch then cast off the first as normal.

Step 2. Rotate the RHN clockwise and back to centre. The yarn should have moved to the back of the work. Knit the next stitch then bind off the first stitch as normal. Repeat Steps 1 and 2 until all stitches have been cast off.

I-cord cast-off

Both cast-on and cast-off plus the i-cord selvedge have been used in the Deft mitts (see Chapter 9: Projects) to create a beautifully crafted edge. This is another cast-off that needs to be worked loosely. Since, you are working perpendicularly to the edge, you are matching rows to stitches and since these are not the same numbers in a knitted gauge, it will give a tighter edge. The easiest method is to go up a few needle sizes. This is especially important if casting off a shawl, as you need the stretch along that cast-off edge. Depending on the pattern, if you have an i-cord selvedge, you can just use these 3 stitches to start. If you don't, then cast on 2 extra stitches.

If working with an i-cord selvedge, continue until 6 stitches remain, then you can seamlessly finish the i-cord by grafting the last 3 stitches together with 3 stitches from the i-cord. Otherwise, continue until 3 stitches remain and slip one, k2tog, pass slipped stitch over (sk2po).

The i-cord cast-off creates a rounded edge that is a match for the i-cord cast-on.

The actual i-cord cast-off is quite simple – k2, ssk, slip 3 stitches back to LHN, rep from * across.

Sewn cast-off (also known as Elizabeth Zimmermann's sewn bind-off)

It does require sewing rather than knitting to create. This method was created by Elizabeth Zimmermann, in an effort to find an alternative cast-off that didn't look like casting off. It creates a stretchy edge with minimal flaring. This technique is relatively simple to execute, as it remains the same for every stitch across the row. Cut the yarn to four times the width of the edge to be bound off and thread onto a darning needle.

The sewn cast-off is one of the stretchiest methods and creates little flare.

STEP-BY-STEP: SEWN CAST-OFF

Step 1. Insert into the first 2 stitches purlwise and pull through.

Step 2. Insert into the first stitch knitwise and remove this stitch from the knitting needle. Repeat these two steps until all stitches have been cast off.

Icelandic cast-off

The Icelandic cast-off is another method that is slightly looser than a traditional cast-off. This is the cast-off that I recommended for my Variegata pattern, as it gives that stretch, yet blends into the garter stitch edge. Start by knitting the first stitch.

This works well with a garter stitch fabric, as the edge blends in well with the garter stitch ridge but has some stretch.

STEP-BY-STEP: ICELANDIC CAST-OFF

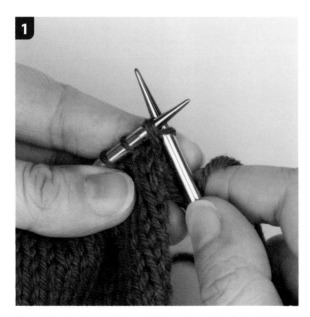

Step 1. Slip back to LHN. Insert RHN purlwise into the just knit stitch and then knitwise into the second stitch and pull this through the centre of the first.

Step 2. Knit this second stitch and drop both from the LHN. Repeat from Step 1 until all stitches have been bound off.

Russian cast-off (also known as decrease cast-off)

This method has many different names, such as lace, Russian, decrease and so on. It is ideal for a stretchy edge such as the top of a sock and it is this method that I've recommended for the Nimble socks (see Chapter 9: Projects). It does create a slightly flared edge compared to the sewn cast-off but is quicker to create. I feel that this compromise balances out well, especially since the top of a sock is worn stretched and the flare isn't noticeable.

- **Knit version:** k1, *k1, slip both stitches back to LHN, k2togtbl, rep from * until all stitches are cast off.
- **Purl version:** p1, *p1, slip both stitches back to LHN, p2tog, rep from * until all stitches are cast off.

A combination of the two can be worked to cast off in a rib pattern for a more streamlined finish. When the next stitch is a knit stitch, work the knit cast-off from * and if it is a purl stitch work the purl version.

The Russian cast-off can be used with a variety of stitches.

1. Knit version.

2. Ribbed version.

3. Purl version.

FINAL STITCH UNTIDINESS

This is one of the first times that I noticed the untidiness of my knitting – that final cast-off stitch can look larger than the rest. The first step is to knit the first stitch of the last row tightly; this will remove some of the excess, but don't worry if you forget as there is another technique.

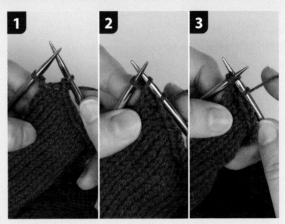

Step 1. Work until the final stitch.

Step 2. Using the LHN, pick up the stitch from the row below from right to left and then slip the final stitch back to the LHN.

Step 3. Knit these two together and cast off as normal. This pulls some of the excess yarn to the back, giving a neater finish.

Top sample is knitted as normal and the final stitch of a cast-off tends to be loose and untidy. The bottom sample has the improved technique.

It's a minor point but when finishing your final cast-off stitch – cut the yarn and then just pull the stitch loop out. Many finish the final cast-off and then thread the yarn through the final live stitch. This just adds an extra stitch to the corner and is unnecessary.

CASTING OFF IN THE ROUND

This is a similar problem to stripes in the round. Since you're not knitting in a perfect concentric circle, but instead you are working in a spiral, the final stitch will sit higher than the first of the round. There are a couple of different techniques to use to level this join for a neat finish.

Knitted join

The knitted join is the quicker but less tidy of the two.

To work, once the final stitch of the round has been cast off, insert the RHN needle underneath the loops of the first stitch that was cast off. Pick up and knit a stitch into these loops and then cast off as normal.

Sewn join

Keep the last stitch live (either on the needle or put a stitch marker in), cut the yarn to 15cm (6in) and thread on a darning needle.

The sewn join is a little slower to create but creates an invisible join.

STEP-BY-STEP: SEWN JOIN

Step 1. Take the yarn from the back to the front through the centre of the first stitch on the round.

Step 2. Then take the needle through the live stitch knitwise.

Step 3. Take from front to back under the two legs of the second cast-off stitch of the round.

Step 4. Finally, take it through the live stitch purlwise. Remove the live stitch from its holder and pull the thread to adjust the sizing and then darn in securely at the back.

CHAPTER 7

FINISHING TOUCHES

W hen you finish your knitting, there's a natural tendency to either rush or not bother with those final finishing touches since the actual knitting is done; but it is at this point that you can elevate your project to give it that professional finish.

SEAMING

There are numerous different methods to sew seams with regular fabrics, but the choices are more limited with a knitted fabric. In my opinion, the two main contenders are mattress stitch (also called ladder stitch) and backstitch.

Comparing mattress and backstitch

Mattress stitch allows you to be precise, as you can work stitch by stitch, matching both sides. You are working from the front of the fabric too, so you can see immediately whether it looks right. If done correctly, you won't be able to see the seam from the front and it gives a neat (though, perhaps rather bulky) seam on the reverse. You can even use a completely contrasting yarn and it won't be visible, so that's useful if you've run out of the main yarn.

It is easier to achieve the perfect finish with mattress stitch. From the front, it looks like the fabric continues across. It has a little give to it, which is often a benefit, as you don't want the seams

Left to right: mattress stitch gives a neat seam. Backstitch gives a strong seam for shoulders.

to distort the fabric. However, very occasionally, you'll want a firm seam to stop the fabric from stretching out.

The other main contender is backstitch. This is done with the right sides of the fabric facing, which means that you can't necessarily see the final finish easily. It is harder to get a perfect finish with backstitch. I find that I can get mattress stitch neat every time but not with backstitch. Often, I have to redo sections that aren't quite neat enough. However, it does give a firmer seam. Shoulder seams, especially with heavyweight garments, can benefit from a backstitch seam over mattress stitch.

They both create similar bulk on the reverse of the fabric. Mattress stitch is what I pull out of my toolkit most often, but it is useful to know how to create a backstitch seam too.

Mattress stitch

Side seams

When joining side seams, it is easier to work when the pieces are worked to exactly the same length. I'd recommend that you work to rows rather than to measurement when you are making matching pieces; for example, when making a sweater, ensure that the front and back have the same number of rows.

You'll find that many beginner tutorials, including the step-by-step images shown in this chapter, will show the fabric pieces both facing upwards, as it's easier to demonstrate to the knitter where to place the needle. However, in practice, it's often easier to hold the fabric in your hands with the wrong sides together. You can manipulate the angle more easily and it feels more natural. It means that you can pin the edges together too, so if they're not quite the same length, you can 'ease' in the longer side. If you know that you have the same number of rows and the seams are straight, you don't necessarily have to pin the edges together. However, it's probably good practice to do this. Use knitters' pins and pin the fabrics wrong sides together. Use as many pins as you feel comfortable with. I don't tend to put too many in – I'd say a bare minimum would be every quarter or every 15cm (6in). When you reach the pins, pull them out before sewing that section.

To start your mattress stitch, cut the yarn about three times the length of the seam to be joined. If it is an excessively long edge, it will be more comfortable to use a shorter length and join in a second strand later. It does give you more options if you use a separate piece of yarn rather than a tail end from a cast-off edge. If the yarn is separate, the mattress stitch can be pulled firmly to remove if you want to redo it. Also, if you want to make any adjustments at a later stage, it allows you to redo the seam from either end.

There are two ways to work mattress stitch; either under 1 row or 2. One row gives a firmer edge, which is also a little bulkier. Working under 2 rows is less bulky and twice as quick to sew. Either is fine, though I always use the 2-row method as it's quicker, less bulky and I've never had any issues with any gaps or untidiness. I will demonstrate the two-row method but feel free to substitute going under 1 row, if you prefer. Using a blunt darning needle, thread the yarn. Make sure to leave a 15cm (6in) tail for sewing in later.

The trick to the tension is to close the seam shut but don't pull it too tightly.

Mattress stitch on side seams gives a seamless finish.

STEP-BY-STEP: MATTRESS STITCH ON SIDE SEAMS

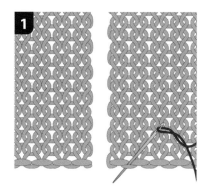

Step 1. Insert the needle from top to bottom into the cast-on edge on the back piece.

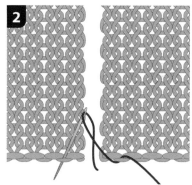

Step 2. Insert the needle from top to bottom into the cast-on edge on the front piece.

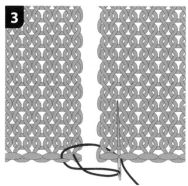

Step 3. Reinsert into the same space that the yarn came out of on the back piece and go up **one** strand/row.

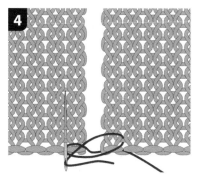

Step 4. Reinsert into the same space that the yarn came out of on the front piece and go up **two** strands/rows.

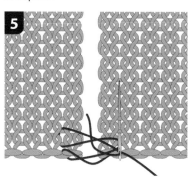

Step 5. Reinsert into the same space that the yarn came out of on the back piece and go up **two** strands.

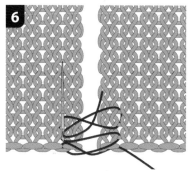

Step 6. Reinsert into the same space that the yarn came out of on the front piece and go up **two** strands. Continue the previous two steps until the seams are joined together.

MATTRESS STITCH POSITIONING

The general rule for positioning is to work one complete stitch in from the edge. However, this can be easily missed as that edge stitch flips around to the back of the fabric. There are two tips that will help you work at the correct point. Firstly, tilt the fabric to look at the reverse regularly and secondly, you can use your finger in between the two pieces to roll the edges out. However, if you miss the correct point, try to keep in the same column for the entire seam as it will give a neater finish.

- If you work a full stitch in on both pieces, the knitted fabric will look seamless.
- If you work one and a half stitches in, then it will still look neat but not a seamless fabric.
- If you are working with a very bulky fabric, then work half a stitch in on each side and there will be a less bulky seam on the reverse.

Mattress stitch worked one and a half stitches in gives a neat but not seamless finish.

Stripes

When seaming stripes, the seam creates a small jog, so it takes some effort to get them to line up. You can always work with trial and error until it lines up correctly, but there are a few tips to get them to marry up perfectly.

The method for mattress stitch (see previous section) where you work across 1 row on the back piece and then 2 on the front lines up the fabric at the correct position. However, if you find that you miss the correct space or, as you continue, it moves out of alignment, then you can move it back quite simply. When you reach your first stripe, ensure that the back piece works the new colour first. If working over 2 rows, make sure the first is a strand of the old colour, then one of the new. On the front piece, both strands should be the new colour. If you are working the one-row method, you should work the new colour on the back piece first.

Top seams

Mattress stitch can be used on both cast-on and cast-off edges. This is the same principle as working grafting top to top. The seam will be offset by half a stitch. As you hold the knitting, you will have the front piece the correct way up, but you'll see the back piece upside down. This means that it will look like you are working in a different position on each piece, but it only appears that way.

A word on tension; to give this seam strength, make sure that you pull the seam closed. Ideally, the yarn used should not be visible. There is enough movement in this method, so that you don't need to tightly close the seam after every stitch, but keep closing it at regular intervals so that you can control the tension.

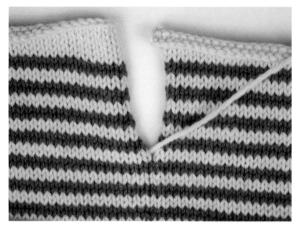

When joining two pieces of fabric that have been worked in stripes, it is possible to get the stripes to marry up perfectly.

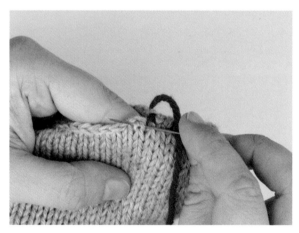

When working mattress stitch at a top seam edge, it appears more reminiscent of grafting than mattress stitch, as you are replicating a knit stitch, though it does work in a similar way to the side seams.

STEP-BY-STEP: MATTRESS STITCH ON TOP SEAMS

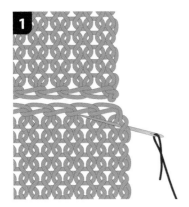

Step 1. Insert the needle from back to front in the front piece through the centre of the **V** of the first stitch.

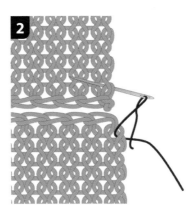

Step 2. Insert the needle from back to front in the back piece through the centre of the first stitch (this can be tricky to see as it rolls to the back).

When working in different stitch patterns such as garter stitch or reverse stocking stitch, the technique is the same – work 1 stitch in from the edge. However, the fabric does look different to stocking stitch as you work.

With reverse stocking stitch, the rows are at the front of the fabric, so you're working under two horizontal bars.

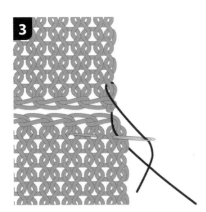

Step 3. Insert on the front piece into the same space that the yarn came out of previously and under two strands (this will be into the centre of one stitch and out of the centre of the next).

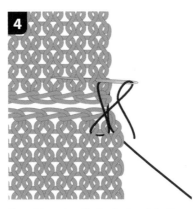

Step 4. Insert on the back piece into the same space that the yarn came out of and under two strands (this will behind both legs of the **V**). Repeat Steps 3 and 4 until the edge has been seamed.

With garter stitch, you're working under an up-and-down ridge.

Backstitch

As mentioned earlier, backstitch can be used inter-changeably with mattress stitch. However, the ideal place is at shoulder seams to give strength, especially when using heavier weight yarns. Backstitch works the same whether it is side or top seams. For side seams, work under both legs of the outer stitch. For top seams, work under both legs of the cast-off stitch.

To work backstitch, place the two pieces right sides together, then:

When working backstitch, have the right sides facing and make sure you go under a full stitch on both pieces.

- **Step 1:** Start at the second stitch in and insert from back to front under both legs of the stitch on the back piece and then the same on the front piece.
- **Step 2:** In the first stitch, insert from front to back on the front piece then the back piece.
- **Step 3:** Working into the next stitch along (for example, the third stitch), insert from back to front under both legs on the back piece then the front.
- **Step 4:** In the previous stitch, insert from front to back on the front piece then the back.
- Repeat the previous two steps along the seam.

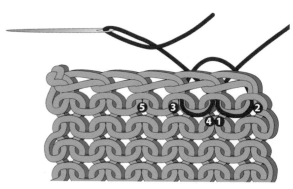

Order of backstitch. The same principle works for side seams, just work under one side stitch instead.

Easing in

Most seams that need to be sewn together will be the same length. However, even if it is meant to be the same length, you might find that either through a sewing or measuring error, you have edges with different lengths. You will need to 'ease in' these sections by working closer together on the shorter side.

For mattress stitch, instead of going up 2 rows on the shorter side, work across 1 row only (whilst maintaining 2 rows on the longer side). Try not to work this too closely together; instead spread this easing evenly along the seam. If you find that you've got near to the end and one edge is a lot longer than the other, then it will be neater to undo the seam a bit and work this easing technique further down the

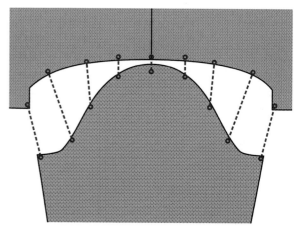

A set-in sleeve is a good example where you need to ease in. To allow for a good fit, the sleeve cap is slightly larger than the armhole. This means that it must be 'eased in' to the armhole.

seam. For back stitch, you can either skip a stitch on the longer side or work into the same stitch again on the shorter side.

Pinning is essential when easing in a shape. To ease in two shapes, fold both pieces in half and pin together at these points. Work across the edge in the same manner, fold both at the quarter points and pin at this point, and so on. When sewing this edge together, you can use mattress stitch with a combination of side and top seam sewing to join them together. Work to each pin and make sure that the fabric is lining up at those points. If it doesn't, then pull back the seam a bit and ease in the edge by working closer together on the shorter side.

WEAVING IN ENDS

This is another area that has many different techniques. If the end stays where it is whilst in use and isn't visible from the front, then the 'weaving in' is doing its job properly. There are a few principles to follow that are helpful for weaving in ends.

- Leave yourself at least 15cm (6in) of yarn to use for weaving in. I've seen many knitters trying to be frugal with short yarn ends but it is really a false economy. Give yourself a few extra inches and make it easier.
- Wait until the end. If you change your mind, make a mistake or just want to redo something, it is far easier to undo your knitting if you haven't already sewn the ends in.
- If working in multiple colours, always work your ends into the same colour yarn, if possible.
- If you have seams in your project, then this is the best place to work the ends in. It's easier and they hide within the bulk of the seam.
- Try not to sew more than one end into the same place. This isn't always possible though.
- Try to travel at least 2.5cm (1in) with your ends.

- Make sure that the end reverses direction at least once.
- Avoid knots.

I touched on this topic in Chapter 4 – when working with more than one yarn and the best ways to join in new yarn. Some of those techniques didn't require any further treatment but some, such as the slip knot join, needs the ends darning in afterwards. If you're not sure whether you need to darn in the ends, then it's better to err on the side of caution and darn them in.

This is one area where many have found their own way by 'just doing' and because of that everyone does it differently. This is the way I do it and it is neither right nor wrong. I do think that knitting shouldn't have rules such as 'you must do this' and 'you must do that' to be right. Knitting is a creative art and it should be what you want it to be. However, if your aim is neatness then I can guide you along the path that I have taken to improve the finish.

Weaving into seams

The first choice with ends will always be to sew it into a seam. It is invisible and the bulk from the seam is already there, so you won't affect the fabric in any way. You could overhand sew over the seam but, in my opinion, this adds to the bulk of the seam. Instead, weave in and out of the seam in a serpentine manner for about 2.5cm (1in) and then reverse direction and come back again.

The sample shown has the serpentine weaving in the centre before it is pulled in. Either side has the weaving pulled in and it's nearly invisible.

Duplicate stitch

If in doubt on how to deal with your ends, you can't go wrong with duplicate stitch; the principle being that you follow the path of the stitches in the fabric on the wrong side. The end sits directly behind the stitch on the front, so it is invisible from the front and maintains the same stretch in the fabric that was already there. The downsides are it does thicken the fabric and it can be a little harder to work on some fabrics.

Using duplicate stitch on the wrong side of reverse stocking stitch is quite easy as you just follow the **V** of the stitch.

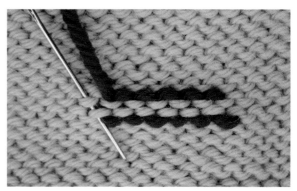

Duplicate stitch on the wrong side of stocking stitch is slightly harder, but just follow the yarn as it moves through the stitches. This is completely invisible from the right side of the work.

Weaving into garter stitch

Garter stitch creates a thick fabric with ridges on each side. This means it is easy to hide ends in the ridges.

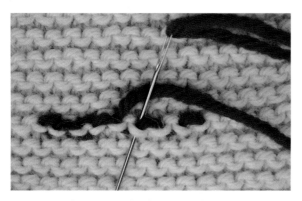

You can treat the garter stitch ridges in a similar manner to the seams and weave in and out of a ridge.

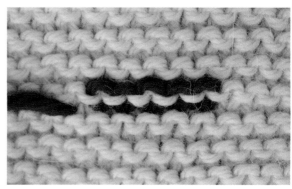

The alternative is to work duplicate stitch, though this can be visible from the front in garter stitch, so only use this if using matching yarn.

Weaving in stocking stitch and reverse stocking stitch

Duplicate stitch gives the best finish in my opinion and will be my first choice on stocking stitch fabric. However, if the yarn is a different colour or it isn't always easy to see where the stitch travels, you can work diagonally instead. When working duplicate stitch, the needle travels underneath the entire thread. However, when working diagonally, skim through half of the yarn across diagonally and then turn a dog leg and work back again.

Another method is to skim diagonally. Just make sure you work backwards too, so the end stays in place.

Weaving in other stitch patterns

Ribbing can be treated like stocking stitch, except try to take the end away from the edge, so it isn't visible from the right side. You can use a combination of skimming and/or duplicate stitch. Another option is to oversew down a knit column but my preference is for the weaving to lie flatter on the wrong side.

Lace knitting can be a little tricky to manage as there are holes to manoeuvre around and sometimes, the fabric can be loose enough that everything is visible. If you can use techniques that blend into the fabric, such as a felted join or Russian join instead, this would be less visible. Alternatively, try and work any ends into areas that have a few knit stitches together and, failing that, follow the duplicate stitch rule and take the ends along the same path as the stitches.

Left: oversewing of knit column. Right: duplicate stitch and skimming.

Left: duplicate stitch following a row of lace knitting. Right: keeping the weaving in to a section of stocking stitch.

BLOCKING

Blocking is that final finishing touch for your project and it really makes a difference. There isn't a project I wouldn't block because when I have put all that time and effort in, I want to see it at its best. The question I always ask is 'are you the sort of person that would wear an unironed shirt?'. If the answer is yes, then maybe you might want to skip this section. If the answer is no, then you'll be far happier with your projects if you block them.

The basic principle of blocking is to add moisture and lay the item into the position that you want it to look like and then let it dry. There are several different ways to go about this and it can depend on the type of project and/or fibre content of the yarn.

Blocking methods

These are the three methods that I would recommend – wet, spray, and steam blocking.

Wet blocking

Wet blocking gives the most dramatic results and is suitable for most fibre types. This method gives the most significant and long-lasting results. However, a word of caution; if you haven't done your preparatory work with your gauge swatch with blocking and hanging it, then you could have an unwanted

Left: unblocked. Right: blocked. Blocking can make a dramatic difference to the finish of your project.

Left : unblocked. Right: blocked. Any project can benefit from being blocked. The Nimble socks (see Projects) look quite different pre- and post-blocking.

surprise with this technique. Some fibre types can change substantially once wet. Superwash wool yarn can grow quite dramatically, and plant-based fibres can shrink.

This technique isn't ideal for silk or novelty yarns either. Silk can become fragile once wet, so if using this fibre then wet block with care. Don't over-stretch or put too much pressure on, as there is the potential for silk to snap when wet. Novelty texture yarns could change texture once wet, so the finished look could be different to what you were aiming for. If unsure, test block a swatch first.

The other downside is when using contrasting colour yarns, for example, red and white, the dye can potentially bleed, so if you think this might be an issue, test block a swatch first. Alternatively, you can mitigate dye bleeding by adding a colour catcher sheet and blocking in cold water and not leaving it to soak for very long. If this looks like a potential issue, then use spray or steam blocking instead. All these issues can be offset if you make a swatch and block this before you start.

Hopefully, I haven't put you off with all the ways it can go wrong. Let's look at how to wet block your projects to show off their full potential. Firstly, soak your project in lukewarm water for about 15 minutes. Many natural fibres can felt. This happens when there is both moisture and friction. We're adding the moisture by wet blocking, so we need to avoid adding friction. Fill your sink/tub first with lukewarm water. If you want to wash it, then I'd rec-ommend adding a no-rinse wool wash, so you don't have to remove the suds afterwards (and avoid cre-ating friction). Now, add your project to the water. Let the water soak up naturally or, if you're impa-tient (like me), very gently press the project down to remove the air bubbles and soak up the water.

Have a large towel on the floor ready for drying. After 15 minutes, hold onto the project so it doesn't move about in the water and drain the sink/tub. Gently **press** into the bottom to remove excess

water – don't wring. Supporting the weight of the project, spread out on the towel. Roll the towel up and stand on it to press out the water. If the project is very large, then it will speed the drying process if you repeat this with a second towel. Again, supporting the weight, lay out the project into the shape that you want (pin or use blockers, see later in the chapter for more details) and leave to dry. Many fibres can feel dry but still contain water, so leave it to dry longer than you think is necessary. This seems like quite a prolonged process but essentially, you're just handwashing your project and laying it out in position to dry.

Steam blocking

Steam blocking is the quickest technique and useful if time is of the essence. The results are not as dramatic as wet blocking but for most projects, it works sufficiently well. However, there are a few fibres not to use this technique with. Angora can felt very easily and the lustre of mulberry silk can be dulled with heat. Artificial fibres that are plastic-based, or blends containing them, can melt with heat. Therefore, steam blocking is not recommended for these fibres.

Use either a steam iron or steamer and hold just above the fabric, about 1cm (½in) away. Often, irons have a button to produce extra steam, so use this. Steam the entire surface and let dry for 10-15 minutes. I'm not one for rules in knitting but this is one I feel passionately about: don't ever allow the iron to make direct contact with your knitting. Yarn has body and air within the fibres and you can easily ruin the handle of the fabric if you iron it.

Spray blocking

Spray blocking is the safety option. If you're unsure about using either of the other two options, then spray block. This can be used with any fibre and you can also avoid colour bleed problems. However, the results are a bit more subdued than wet blocking.

Lay out the item in position using any blocking aids, such as pins or wires, that you want. Make sure that you use a waterproof surface, such as blocking pads. Use a spray bottle filled with water. Heavily spray the surface of the project and then let dry. If using this technique on double-sided items, such as garments or cowls, you'll need to repeat this for the other side. However, spray blocked items dry far quicker than wet blocked ones.

Artificial fibres

Artificial fibres such as acrylic, don't produce as long-lasting or pronounced results as natural fibres when blocked. Plastics behave differently with water than other materials. However, it does improve the fabric and is still worth doing, as it relaxes any odd shapes. Many will recommend 'setting' acrylic by steam blocking. However, acrylic is plastic and you're effectively melting it and this will change the handle of the fabric. It isn't something that I would recommend, as you've put all that effort into the knitting and then you're melting it and it's not something you can reverse if you dislike it.

Table 2   Suitable blocking methods for different yarns and fibres

Yarn types and fibres	Suitable for wet blocking?	Suitable for steam blocking?	Suitable for spray blocking?
Wool	Yes	Yes	Yes
Alpaca	Yes	Yes	Yes
Mohair	Yes	Yes	Yes
Cashmere	Yes	Yes	Yes
Angora	With caution. Can easily felt	Not recommended	Yes
Linen	Yes	Yes	Yes
Cotton	Yes	Yes	Yes
Silk	With caution. Can become easy to break when wet	Not recommended	Yes
Artificial fibres	Yes	Not recommended	Yes
Blends	Yes	Not recommended, if contains artificial fibres	Yes
Novelty	Yes	Not recommended	Maybe. Test with a swatch first

Pinning

In principle, you can just lay an item out flat and let it dry. However, it will shrink back again. If you're looking for exact results or trying to open up a lace pattern, you can stop this shrinkage and movement if you pin the item into shape first. That way it will look exactly as you pin it once it is dry.

There are a number of tools that can make blocking easier but the bare basics that you need are pins and a surface to block on. T-pins are ideal but other pins will do the same job, though it's probably wise to use stainless steel ones to stop any rust marks.

Blocking mats are foam blocks that interlock with each other so that you can create the shape of your item. Children's play mats or workshop flooring are the same thing, so you can use those too. Another option is to block on the floor but put something down, such as a towel, to protect the floor from moisture and any potential colour bleeding. There are lots of other tools available to make blocking a quicker and easier process, but if you have pins and a base to block on to, then you can block anything.

The finished item will look exactly how it is pinned once dry; so if you've pinned with a wavy edge or scallops, then that is how it will look once the pins have been removed. Ensure that it looks how you want before you leave it to dry.

If you have a long straight edge, then you can pin out with care but try to keep the pins close together, so that you don't create an unwanted scalloped edge. However, if the edge is quite long, blocking wires would be a better option.

The ideal type of pin is a stainless-steel T-pin, since they won't rust when wet and the T-shape stops the knitting sliding off the pin.

If you have ribbed edge or any other area that needs to remain elastic, then don't pin or stretch that out. Let it dry to its natural position and it will retain its elasticity.

There are specialized blockers on the market that are a series of pins attached to a plastic handle. This makes straight edges easier and quicker to pin plus you can avoid a scalloped edge.

Blocking wires

Blocking wires can speed up the blocking process and allow you to avoid undesirable scalloped edges. There are two main types: stiff and flexible. The stiff ones are ideal for straight edges.

For the neatest finish, try to weave blocking wires in the same manner every time, for example, from front to back into the edge stitches or weave into alternate stitches. Try to place the wires into every stitch or every other stitch, as this will give a more uniform edge. As with all things knitting, whatever you choose to do – be consistent. If you have an intentional scallop edge, such as a shawl, then the wires can be placed into the tips of the scallops only. Once the wires are in place then stretch the wires out into the position that you want and pin them at intervals to keep them in position. If you have an item with a curved edge, such as a crescent shawl, then straight wires won't be as easy to use. This is where flexible wires can be helpful.

Heddle is a crescent-shaped shawl with a picot edge, so I used flexible wires through each picot and pinned the wire into a gentle curve.

If you are blocking a double-sided item, such as the Dapper Spruce cowl, then you can place the wires inside and use them to stretch the item from the inside. Once stretched out, just pin them at intervals through the fabric to keep them in position.

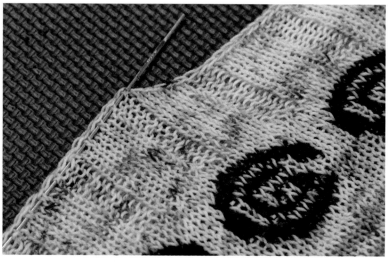

If the item is single-sided, then they can be woven along the edge.

Other blocking tools

There are different blocking forms that you can buy for quick and easy blocking; the most common being the sock blocker. This is a sock-shape that can be created from any sort of material – I own them in plastic, metal, and wood. The item is then placed on the blocker to dry. My preference for formers like this is to have some sort of opening in the centre, as it allows the item to dry quickly. Mitten blockers are readily available too.

However, you might find that you have an item that isn't a flat shape, so you sometimes have to think outside the box for the best way to give the item its natural shape as it dries. Hats are a good example. My go-to for hat blocking is to blow up a balloon to the required head size and let the hat dry on that. This works particularly well, since the ribbing is left unstretched allowing it to remain elastic.

If you have a tam or beret-shape, then using a plate would work better. Over the years, I've used all sorts of household items to get the shape that I want.

Another option is to create your own blockers by using thin plastic. You can buy specific template plastic, but children's plastic placemats are similar. Just cut out your required shape and place inside your item. I used homemade plastic blockers when blocking the Deft mitts. They are designed to be ergonomically shaped to your wrist, so the edges are not straight. Using homemade blockers allowed me to create the perfect shape for the mitts. However, if you don't have the right shape or the ability to make your own, then just laying an item flat to dry will do a good job of blocking. If you find that you have an unwanted fold line once it has dried, you can steam or spray block just the fold again to remove it.

Blocking toolkit

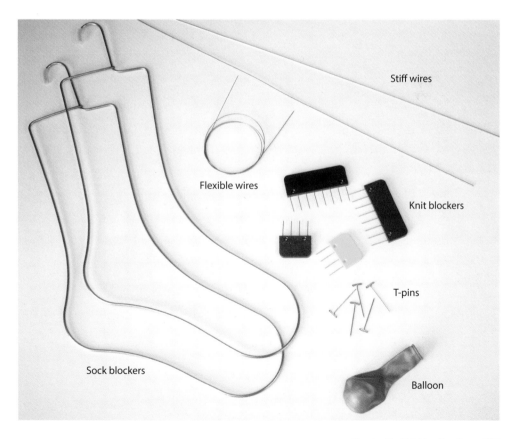

Stiff wires

Flexible wires

Knit blockers

T-pins

Sock blockers

Balloon

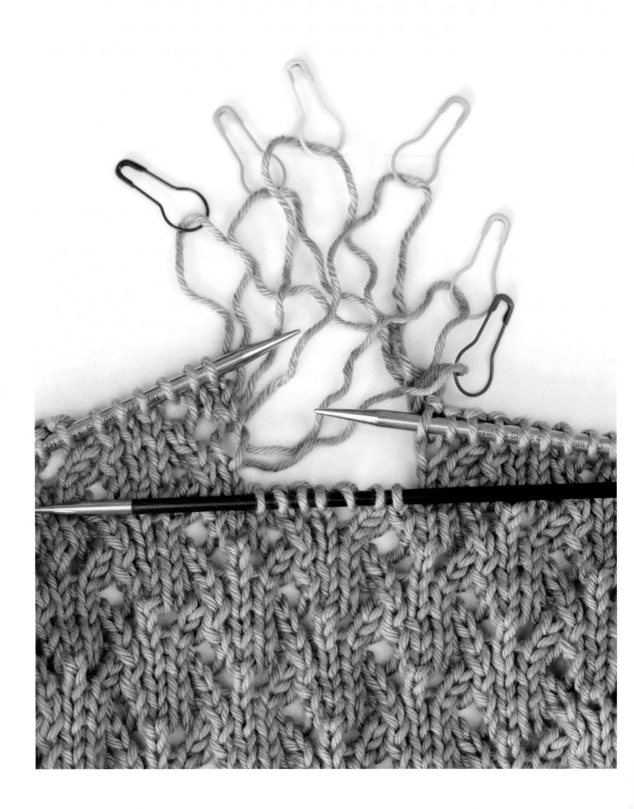

CHAPTER 8

TROUBLESHOOTING

To err is human. With the best will in the world, we all make mistakes in our knitting. The one beauty of knitting compared to other crafts is the yarn is not 'consumed' as you use it. It can be pulled back and reknitted. Often, I have knitters bring me knitting for me to fix or to provide guidance on the best way to sort it themselves. Sometimes, it's obvious what the issue is but surprisingly often, they spend time trying to 'find' the mistake. If you can't find it easily, no one is going to notice except you. It depends on your desire for perfection, but if you can't spot it easily then leave it – but if it's going to annoy you and there isn't an easy fix, just reknit it. Hopefully, we all knit because we enjoy it, so if you enjoyed it the first time then you'll probably also enjoy the process the second time.

It's easier to fix issues if you spot them quickly rather than later, with many rows of knitting between you and the mistake; so try and look at your fabric regularly to check. It is possible to fix them at the later stage, but this requires more work; whether it's dropping the stitches all the way down, reknitting the piece or using grafting/sewing to solve the issue.

CHECKLIST FOR SPOTTING A MISTAKE

Sometimes, we know there's something not quite right in our knitting, such as the pattern isn't lining up or there are not enough stitches to finish a repeat, but trying to figure out where the mistake is can be frustrating. Try following this checklist in order and you should be able to track it down with less frustration:

1. Scan your knitting and see if you can spot any dropped stitches.
2. Check your stitch count and see if it matches the pattern.
3. If your stitch count is wrong, check that all increases and decreases are done where they should have been.
4. See if the pattern lines up with previous rows.
5. Examine the row on the needles and follow the instructions and check each stitch has been done according to the pattern.
6. Failing all that, check down your work for a row that you know is correct and take the knitting back to that point.

READING YOUR KNITTING

There's one very important skill for a knitter to learn that can make a huge difference to the process – reading your knitting. If you can recognize what stitch is on your needle, how to count rows and see where an increase/decrease is within the fabric, then you won't lose track and you can fix mistakes easily. This skill comes naturally with practice, but I'm going to show you some of the basics to get you started.

If you encounter a new stitch, then see what it looks like just after it's been worked and again on the subsequent row. If you take the time to do this, then your skill with reading your knitting will get a jump start. If you struggle with this, consider taking a photo of the stitches instead and you can refer back to it later.

Counting rows

Being able to count your rows in knitting can be a useful tool. I tend not to mark off rows on my pattern and instead read my knitting and count rows to see where I am. This means that I'm not beholden to my pattern, row counter or pen and paper. Instead, I can be engrossed in my knitting. This is where stitch markers can be useful. Being able to keep track between increases or decreases makes shaping more

A knit stitch is a loop of yarn and when it sits below the knitting needle then it looks like a V.

A purl stitch is the wrong side of this loop and will look like a bump sitting directly under the needle.

Decreases will have the two overlapping stitches directly under the needle.

There is such a variety of increases that they look different next to the needle, but the make one increase looks like this.

enjoyable. I tend to just count the rows as I recognize what the decrease looks like in my knitting, but if you are still learning to recognize this, then just pop a stitch marker through your decrease once you've completed it instead.

After knitting 2 rows past your cast-on, it should be easy to recognize what part of your knitting is your cast-on row. This helps later to know where to start counting from. If you're still unsure, place a stitch marker in the cast-on row and you'll know where to start from. Just remember that the stitches on your needle count as a row of knitting.

If you need to provide yourself somewhere to start your row count from, but the stitch pattern has remained the same, then place a stitch marker in the fabric to give yourself a landmark to start from, for example, the length of a sock foot or armhole.

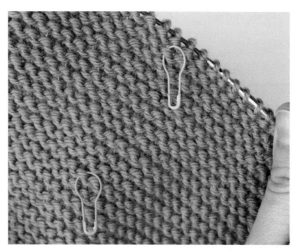

When counting rows then I'll place a mark in the fabric every 20 rows, that way I'm not constantly recounting.

HELPFUL TOOLS FOR TROUBLESHOOTING

Stitch markers

I'm a huge fan of lockable stitch markers. There are so many ways that they can make knitting easier. As I mentioned earlier, they are helpful for marking landmark points and counting rows. They can also be helpful when trying to fix mistakes.

When counting rows, learn to recognize what your cast-on looks like. The easiest way to do this is to work your cast-on and the first 2 rows then get your bearings with how that looks.

Marking mistakes

If you find a dropped stitch, put a stitch marker into the stitch to stop it dropping further. If you find a mistake, such as a split stitch further down, mark the column that the mistake is in by placing a stitch marker in the top stitch of the column on the needle. This can be a lifesaver. It stops you having to slip all the stitches to that position, and instead you can fix it as you work past it. I've done this on occasion and put my project aside for months. Upon returning, that stitch marker told me there was something that I needed to fix. Otherwise, I would have happily knitted on and been even more frustrated later.

Use stitch markers to mark mistakes that need fixing. When you reach the marker, then you can sort the problem.

When dropping a stitch down to fix, I'll place a stitch marker into the stitch below the mistake, so it won't run any further than I want. This is essential when working with multiple columns, such as when fixing a mistake below a decrease.

Pattern repeats

Stitch markers can be useful when placed between pattern repeats. It can help you spot the mistake; for example, if you are working an 8-stitch repeat and you know there is a mistake somewhere. Count the stitches between the markers and if there aren't 8 stitches, then you know the exact section where the problem is and you can then fix it accordingly.

Lifelines

If you're trying a new technique, then lifelines are a good idea. There are a couple of ways to put in a lifeline. Basically, a row of stitches is threaded onto a lifeline, and this means that if something goes wrong then you can take the knitting off your needle and the lifeline will hold the stitches and stop them from running any further down. You can then return them to your needle safely and try again.

Proactive lifelines

Proactive lifelines are put in before you have an issue, so if you're not confident about the next step or the technique is a new one, then use a lifeline before continuing. Before adding a lifeline, ensure that everything is correct on your current row and double check your stitch count.

The first method for inserting a lifeline is to thread this onto a darning needle and take the needle through the centre of every stitch across the row. Ensure your lifeline is long enough, so you can tie the ends together without restricting the fabric. That way it won't interfere or come out by accident. When working the next row, try to avoid knitting the lifeline into the stitches. The second method only works if you are using interchangeable needles.

Using stitch markers between repeats can help you keep track across the row, and you'll quickly notice if you've veered off as the pattern repeat won't end at the marker.

When inserting a lifeline, use a smooth thread smaller than your needle size, such as sock yarn, dental floss or sewing thread.

Most interchangeable needles have a small hole at the base of the needle for tightening the tips to the cables. Insert the lifeline through this hole (it will have to be small enough to fit, so a thinner thread is better) and then work your next row. Pull the needle through, so that the hole is past the stitches and remove the thread from the hole. The lifeline should be sitting through the centre of all your stitches.

Reactive lifelines

Lifelines can be added to your knitting at a later stage too. Using thread and a darning needle, instead of working into the stitches of the current row, thread into a row lower down in the fabric.

Another method is to use a knitting needle. A thinner needle than the one you are working with makes it easier. Work in the same manner as with the thread and darning needle and pick up the right-hand leg of every stitch.

FIXING MISTAKES WHILST KNITTING

Fixing mistakes without reknitting

If you have a mistake that is below the needles, then it is possible to fix this without taking the knitting down. The nearer it is to the needle, the quicker it is to fix. However, it is also possible to fix a mistake all the way at the beginning. If the mistake is within a few rows of the needles, you can use the needle tips to fix the mistake. If it is further down, a crochet hook is more manageable. Use one that is slightly smaller than the size you are working with to make it easier. If the mistake is across a large section of stitches, you can drop that section of stitches down instead and reknit it.

To insert a reactive lifeline, insert the darning needle under the right-hand leg of every stitch in the row.

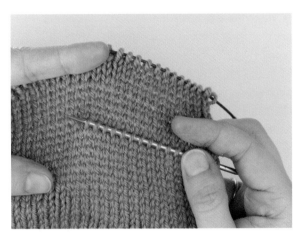

Using a knitting needle as a reactive lifeline can be more useful, as a reactive lifeline is often needed if you want to take the knitting back.

STEP-BY-STEP: PICKING UP A STOCKING STITCH

If the mistake is within reach of the needle tips, you can pick up dropped knit stitches easily with the needles.

Step 1. Insert the RHN from front to back into the dropped stitch (making sure that it isn't twisted).

Step 2. Insert the RHN under the strand from the next row up. Pass the stitch on the needle over the strand as if casting off. Repeat this until the entire column is fixed.

If the mistake is further down, use a crochet hook instead. After fixing each row, the hook should be in the stitch in the correct position ready to fix the next row. Continue in this manner until the whole column is fixed.

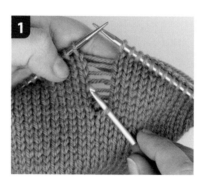

Step 1. Insert the crochet hook from front to back into the stitch (without twisting it).

Step 2. Insert the hook under the strand from the next row up. Rotate the hook to catch the strand and pull it through the stitch.

STEP-BY-STEP: PICKING UP A PURL STITCH

If working in reverse stocking stitch, it is easier to work from the wrong side of the work, so that you see the knit side of the fabric and work in the same manner as for stocking stitch. However, you might want to fix a purl stitch with the needle tips, so you don't need to turn the work.

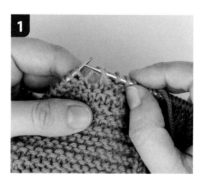

Step 1. Insert the RHN from back to front into the stitch. The strand for the next row should be at the front of the work; insert the RHN under this strand.

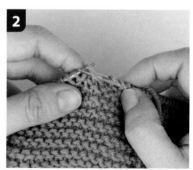

Step 2. Pass the stitch over this strand and then repeat until the entire column is corrected.

Picking up in twisted rib

Insert the hook into the stitch from back to front, then rotate the hook clockwise away from you (ensuring that the right leg of the stitch has crossed over the left). With the hook facing down, place it over the top of the strand for the next row. Without rotating the hook, scoop the strand through the stitch. The stitch on the hook should be twisted and then repeat until the entire column is fixed.

Picking up in garter stitch

It is harder to fix garter stitch without removing the hook after every stitch. It is possible by inserting the hook between all the front and back strands but I think it is easier to fix garter stitch one stitch at a time.

Firstly, you need to spot which row of garter stitch that you are on. If the next strand is at the front of the work, you need to pick up in purl and if the next strand is at the back of the work, then you need to pick up in knit.

For example, if the first stitch to pick up is a knit stitch, then insert the hook from front to back, and hook the strand through. As in step 1 of the step-by-step sequence, remove the hook from the stitch, reinsert from the back to the front and pull through the strand at the front to pick up in purl. Keep alternating between knit and purl until the entire column is fixed.

It is possible to pick up in twisted rib without having to remove the crochet hook from the stitch after every stitch.

WIGGLE FACTOR

Not necessarily the technical term, but it describes the situation well. If your stitches are messy, uneven, or lopsided, you can fix this with a little bit of wiggling. Use the tip of a needle to wiggle any excess yarn into the neighbouring stitches.

- If a stitch is lopsided, move some of the excess from the longer side into the shorter side.
- If you have a loose stitch, move the excess into the neighbouring stitches.
- If you have a lot of excess yarn and you're not far from the current yarn position, then you can move the excess all the way back to the working yarn.

STEP-BY-STEP: PICKING UP PURL STITCHES IN GARTER STITCH

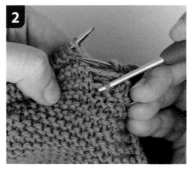

To pick up for the purl stitches in garter stitch.
Step 1. Insert the hook from back to front into the stitch.

Step 2. Take the hook over the top of the strand and scoop through.

Fixing larger mistakes

If you have a larger mistake further down, you can reknit sections. Often, it is easier to keep track if you can pull down an entire pattern repeat. This is important if fixing lace, as the increases and decreases cause the columns to move across the repeat, so you need to ensure that you drop all the stitches that are involved across the mistake.

When I've seen others fixing larger mistakes, they will often pin each row to a mat, so that you make sure that you are using the correct strand for each row. This does restrict your hold on the needles.

It is far easier to do this using the continental method (see Chapter 1), as you don't need to hold as much yarn in your hand for this method. When you get towards the end of the strand, you won't have enough yarn to knit with. Instead, treat the last few stitches as dropped stitches instead. You might have to employ a bit of the 'wiggle factor' when reknitting sections as the edges won't have the same tension as your normal knitting. Move any yarn from loose stitches into the neighbouring ones.

Pulling back your work

Sometimes, the only option to fix a mistake is to pull back your work. You can do this slowly, one stitch at a time. This is called tinking or 'knit' backwards. This is useful when the mistake is within a row or two of your current position. Just remove the yarn from each stitch, one at a time, and return the stitch to the needle.

If you need to pull back a large section, then you can just remove the needle and pull the knitting down. This is called 'frogging', as you 'rip it' back – or, as the frog goes 'ribbit, ribbit'. You can then just return the live stitches to the needle as you reach the required row. This can get a bit messy, as you have less control of stitches dropping down. If you've used this method, then I'd advise just getting a stitch from each column on the needle. They don't necessarily have to be the same row. If you start trying

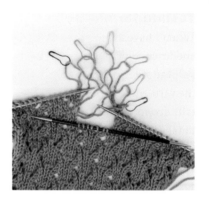

To stop yourself from being restricted, use different coloured stitch markers on each row, so you know which strand to use next.

Using double-pointed needles, reknit each row according to the pattern.

to get the correct row on the needle before the next is on, then you can cascade the problem across the row as the next stitch will often be pulled out. It's far easier to get every column on the needle and then work across the row pulling up any dropped stitches.

However, for more control, when pulling back large sections, use the reactive lifeline mentioned in the above section. You won't have as many dropped stitches to deal with. Should you find that you've used this method but made an error and moved to the next row up or down when picking up, don't worry. This is far easier to deal with than having all the stitches off the needle. Just work across the row and either drop or pick up to make sure they are all from the correct row. This is far quicker and less stressful than having all the stitches off the needle.

Testing for new techniques

When I have a new stitch that I want to understand and learn how to correct on the needles, then I'll knit the stitch and then drop it slowly and see where the yarn enters and leaves. For example, I accidentally dropped a German short row, and I didn't want to take the knitting back. Instead, I worked another German short row into my knitting and then deconstructed it, so I learnt how to put it back together again. You can do this with any stitch and work it out on the needles.

FIXING MISTAKES AT THE END

If you've not spotted the mistake until the end of your knitting, it can be quite disheartening to have to reknit a big chunk of the project. There are many errors that can be fixed or, at the least, improved after the knitting is complete.

Blocking

As mentioned in Chapter 7, blocking can be used to improve the look of the piece. If I'm unhappy with something within a project, I'll block the work before attempting any significant fixing. It's surprising how often blocking will sort out the issue. Knitting has inherent energy from both the stitches and the yarn; blocking smooths this out. Try blocking before anything else, if size or shape are the issue.

Ends

Where there has been picking up of stitches, there can be a tendency for holes to appear. It's possible to avoid these in the first place but if you've only spotted the issue at the end, then you can use the ends to improve the look. Armholes and thumbs are common areas where these holes can happen and, often, these areas will have the yarn joined in at this point too. You can use these ends to improve the holes. Either sew the holes closed, or if possible, use duplicate stitch within these sections to create a stitch.

You can use ends to improve the look of the fabric. If you find that you have holes after picking up for the thumb of Deft, then use the ends to neaten the gap.

Erroneous stitches

Dropped stitches

Finding a dropped stitch after you've cast off can be really frustrating. If it's near the top, you can undo the cast-off and pick up the dropped stitch; this will give the neatest finish. However, if you haven't noticed the dropped stitch for some time or after you've finished, there won't be enough slack to pick the stitch up. Fixing the dropped stitch with this technique makes it appear as part of a decrease instead.

STEP-BY-STEP: FIXING DROPPED STITCHES

Step 1. Use a separate piece of yarn (in the same colour as the surrounding stitches, if possible) and a darning needle, then enter the stitch from the reverse, leaving a tail.

Step 2. Take the needle behind both legs of the top of the stitch to the left.

Step 3. Take the needle behind this stitch and come out between this stitch and the dropped stitch.

Step 4. Take the needle from front to back into the dropped stitch and then duplicate weave in on the reverse. Do the same for the beginning tail.

Using this technique makes the dropped stitch look like part of a decrease stitch.

Yarnovers

Accidental yarnovers can be quite blatant in the fabric. This technique changes open holes to look similar to a closed increase instead.

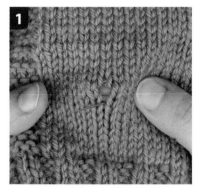

Step 1. Using a darning needle and matching yarn, from the back of the work bring the needle under the strand, beneath the hole from back to front. Leave a tail for darning in later.

Step 2. Then take the needle under the two legs of the stitch above, from right to left.

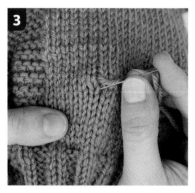

Step 3. Take the needle back down into the same space as it first came out of. Duplicate weave the ends at the back of the work.

Using this technique will make it look like a closed increase instead of an open hole.

Ladders

You can get ladders in your knitting. The worst contenders for this are between needle joins when working in the round or on the right-hand side of a left-leaning decrease. Either employ the 'wiggle factor', or, if they are particularly large, you can improve the look by treating them like a dropped stitch.

After fixing the ladder then, to secure this 'dropped stitch', use a separate piece of yarn in a colour that matches the current position and treat it as a dropped stitch as in the above section. This technique won't give a perfect finish, but it can dramatically improve the look of the fabric.

STEP-BY-STEP: FIXING LADDERS

Step 1. Starting at the bottom of the ladder and using a crochet hook, insert from back to front under an unobtrusive strand.

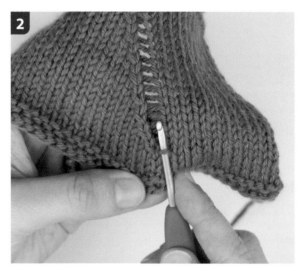

Step 2. Rotate so the hook is facing away from you. This creates a twisted loop like a backward loop increase.

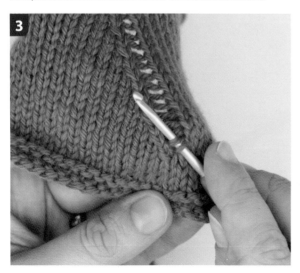

Step 3. Pick up the strands above, as if it were a dropped stitch.

Step 4. When you get to the top of the ladder, you need to treat the loop on the hook like a dropped stitch.

Reknitting without frogging

Some mistakes are bigger than a single stitch. Sometimes, the dimensions are wrong – it will be too long or short. It is possible to fix these larger errors after the end of the project by using a combination of techniques that I've already discussed. As previously mentioned, you can improve sizing and shape with blocking, so do this first to see if it's still an issue after blocking. If it is, you might want to work some more fundamental changes by putting the relevant section back on the needles and adding or removing length.

It depends on whether you want to make changes within a section of knitting or at the edge. If it's within a section, you'll need to put the stitches at the top and bottom of this section on needles. If it's just at one end, then you'll only need to do this at the one side. As in reactive lifelines (see earlier in the chapter) or returning a provisional cast-on to the needles (see Chapter 5), pick up the right leg of all the stitches on the row to return them to the needles.

So you can add or remove rows, you need to separate the row picked up from the rest of the work.

After undoing that first row if you're trying to undo from below and your fabric is stocking stitch, reverse stocking stitch or garter stitch, from that point the yarn will unravel easily if you need it. However, if the pattern changes from knit to purl across the row, this will have to be pulled through each stitch individually and won't unravel. If you have a large section of knit and purl that needs to be removed, it can be easier to cut the yarn near the needles and remove the section instead of trying to unravel it.

If working from the bottom of the stitches as in a provisional cast-on, the stitches will be offset by half a stitch. To avoid a visual jog, try to change to a different stitch pattern, for example, if you need to make a section longer, change to the edging stitch, such as ribbing, and work this longer rather than lengthen the body fabric.

Once you've added or removed the section, you need to finish it off. If you are working at one end, you can just cast off. If you are working within a section, use the grafting technique from Chapter 5 to rejoin the knitting from both needles.

To separate the rows, then cut the yarn on the row just above the needles. Using a separate needle, unthread that row by pulling it through each stitch.

CHAPTER 9

PROJECTS

The following projects use a variety of techniques demonstrated throughout the book. Each pattern has the techniques listed at the start.

NIMBLE SOCKS

Gauge

◆ 34 stitches by 52 rounds = 10cm (4in) in stocking stitch. Check your gauge.

Needles and accessories

◆ 2.25mm (US Size 1) needles for working in the round in preferred method for circular knitting; or size to obtain gauge.
(**Note:** It is difficult to start a toe-up sock on DPNs as the initial rounds are very tight to work on DPNs; preferably work these initial rows on a circular needle and change to DPNs afterwards).
◆ Cable needle
◆ Stitch markers × 2
◆ Darning needle

Nimble is a toe-up sock using lace and cable stitches.

Nimble uses German short rows and increases to create a heel flap and gusset for a well-fitting heel.

Yarn

- Coopknits Socks Yeah (50g; 212m [232yds]; 75 per cent wool, 25 per cent nylon) 4-ply/fingering weight; colourway: Chryso;
- For UK Size 5 (US Size 7): 280 [320, 350, 400] m/306 [350, 384, 438]yd
- For UK Size 11 (US Size 12): 310 [355, 385, 440] m/339 [388, 421, 481]yd

Size

- Small, [Medium, Large, Extra Large]
- To fit 18 [20.5, 23, 25.5]cm/7 [8, 9, 10]in foot circumference.
- Finished dimensions = 15.5 [18, 20.5, 23]cm/ 6 [7, 8, 9]in circumference at foot.

Special abbreviations

- **m1p** – make one purl: insert left-hand needle under the strand between needles from back to front and purl through the front loop (this will be tight because the strand needs to be twisted).
- **pm** – place marker.
- **sm** – slip marker A or B.
- **2/2 LC** – 2 by 2 Left Cross: slip next 2 stitches purlwise to cable needle, and leave at front of work, k2, then k2 from cable needle.
- **2/2 RC** – 2 by 2 Right Cross: slip next 2 stitches purlwise to cable needle, and leave at back of work, k2, then k2 from cable needle.
- **2/1 LC** – 2 by 1 Left Cross: slip next 2 stitches purlwise to cable needle, and leave at front of work, k1, then k2 from cable needle.
- **2/1 RC** – 2 by 1 Right Cross: slip next stitch purlwise to cable needle, and leave at back of work, k2, then k1 from cable needle.
- **2/1 LPC** – 2 by 1 Left Purl Cross: slip next 2 stitches purlwise to cable needle, and leave at front of work, p1, then k2 from cable needle.
- **2/1 RPC** – 2 by 1 Right Purl Cross: slip next stitch purlwise to cable needle, and leave at back of work, k2, then p1 from cable needle.

- **2/2 LPC Special** – 2 by 2 Left Purl Cross Special: slip next 2 stitches purlwise to cable needle, and leave at front of work, p1, k1, then k1, p1 from cable needle.
- **GSR** – German short row: see Abbreviations.

Techniques used

- Judy's magic cast-on (Chapter 2)
- Increases (Chapter 3)
- German short rows (Chapter 3)
- Knit to purl yarnovers (Chapter 3)
- Russian cast-off (Chapter 6)

Instructions

Toe

- Using Judy's magic cast-on, cast on 12 [12, 12, 16] sts.
- **Round 1:** knit.
- **Increase round 2:** *k1, m1l, k4 [4, 4, 6], m1r, k1, pm, rep from * once more – 16 [16, 16, 20] sts. (**Note:** first marker placed is mA, second marker is mB and indicates the start of the round.)
- **Increase round 3:** *k1, m1l, knit to 1 st before mA/B, m1r, k1, smA/B, rep from * once more – 20 [20, 20, 24] sts.
- Rep Increase Round 3 until there are 28 [32, 36, 40] sts.
- **Next round:** knit.
- **Next round:** rep Increase Round 3 once – 32 [36, 40, 44] sts.
- Rep previous 2 rounds until there are 52 [60, 68, 76] sts.

Foot

- **Round 1:** p1 [3, 1, 3], *k2, p2, rep from * 0 [0, 1, 1] more times, k4, (p3, k2) twice, k2, **p2, k2, rep from ** 0 [0, 1, 1] more times, p1 [3, 1, 3], smA, knit to end.
- **Round 2:** p1 [3, 1, 3], *k2tog, yo, p2, rep from * 0 [0, 1, 1] more times, k4, p3, k2tog, yo, p3, k4, **p2,

k2tog, yo, rep from ** 0 [0, 1, 1] more times, p1 [3, 1, 3], smA, knit to end.

- **Round 3:** rep Round 1 once.
- **Round 4:** work next round of Nimble chart (starting with Round 1) until mA, smA, knit to end.
- Rep Round 4 until work measures 7 [7, 8, 8] cm/2.75 [2.75, 3, 3]in shorter than desired foot length. **Note:** once Rounds 1–20 of Nimble chart have been completed, start again at Round 1.

Gusset

- **Increase round 1:** work next round of Nimble Chart, smA, k1, m1l, knit to last st, m1r, k1 – 54 [62, 70, 78] sts.
- **Round 2:** work next round of Nimble Chart, smA, knit to end.
- Rep Rounds 1 and 2 another 12 [12, 12, 13] times – 78 [86, 94, 104] sts in total.
- There should be 26 [30, 34, 38] sts on the instep (top of the foot) and 52 [56, 60, 66] sts on the bottom of the foot.

Heel

- **Row 1 (RS):** work next round of Nimble chart (**note:** make a note of the round, as you'll continue on in pattern at the leg and place these 26 [30, 34, 38] sts on hold whilst working the heel), smA, k33 [36, 39, 44], m1l, GSR, (there should be 18 [19, 20, 21] unworked sts before mB).
- **Row 2 (WS):** p15 [17, 19, 23], m1p, GSR, (there should be 18 [19, 20, 21] unworked sts before mA).
- **Row 3:** k to 2 sts before GSR stitch from previous row, m1l, GSR; (**note:** each double GSR stitch will be separated by a knit stitch).
- **Row 4:** p to 2 sts before GSR stitch from previous row, m1p, GSR.
- Rep Rows 3 and 4 another 3 [4, 5, 5] times – 88 [98, 108, 118] sts. There should 5 [6, 7, 7] double GSR stitches on either side of the heel at this point.

Heel flap

Note: work the double GSR sts as 1 st.

- **Row 1:** k16 [18, 20, 24], ssk (**note:** this ssk will be with the final GSR and next k st), turn;
- **Row 2:** sl 1, p24 [28, 32, 36], p2tog (**note:** this p2tog will be with the final GSR and next p st), turn;
- **Row 3:** (sl 1, k1) to 2 sts before the gap, sl 1, ssk, turn;
- **Row 4:** sl 1, p to 1 st before the gap, p2tog, turn;
- Rep Rows 3 and 4 another 15 [16, 17, 18] more times – 54 [62, 70, 78] sts.
- **Next round:** (sl 1, k1) to 2 sts before the gap, sl 1, ssk, smB, continue working in the round, work next round of Nimble chart, smA, k2tog, knit to end – 52 [60, 68, 76] sts.

Leg

- **Round 1:** work next round of Nimble chart, smA, knit to end.
- Rep Round 1 until leg measures 11.5 [11.5, 14, 14] cm/4.5 [4.5, 5.5, 5.5]in from top of heel flap or until desired length ending with a Round 2, 4, 6, 8, 19 or 20.

Cuff

- **Round 1:** (k 0 [1, 0, 1], p1 [2, 1, 2], *k2, p2, rep from * 0 [0, 1, 1] more times, k4, (p3, k2) twice, k2, **p2, k2, rep from ** 0 [0, 1, 1] more time, p1 [2, 1, 2], k 0 [1, 0, 1]) twice.
- Rep Round 1 until cuff measures 3.75cm/1½in or until desired length.
- Cast off all stitches using the Russian cast-off as follows:
- k1, *k1, slip both stitches back to LHN, k2togtbl, rep from * until all stitches are cast off.
- Darn in all ends and block.

Charted instructions

See Nimble chart for relevant size.

Written instructions

Round 1: p1 [3, 1, 3], *yo, ssk, p2, rep from * 0 [0, 1, 1] more times, 2/2 LC, p3, yo, ssk, p3, 2/2 RC, **p2, yo, ssk, rep from ** 0 [0, 1, 1] more times, p1 [3, 1, 3].

Round 2: p1 [3, 1, 3], *k2, p2, rep from * 0 [0, 1, 1] more times, k4, (p3, k2) twice, k2, **p2, k2, rep from ** 0 [0, 1, 1] more times, p1 [3, 1, 3].

Round 3: p1 [3, 1, 3], *k2tog, yo, p2, rep from * 0 [0, 1, 1] more times, k4, p3, k2tog, yo, p3, k4, **p2, k2tog, yo, rep from ** 0 [0, 1, 1] more times, p1 [3, 1, 3].

Round 4: rep Round 2.

Rounds 5–8: rep Rounds 1–4 once.

Rounds 9–10: rep Rounds 1 and 2 once.

Round 11: p1 [3, 1, 3], *k2tog, yo, p2, rep from * 0 [0, 1, 1] more times, k2, 2/1 LC, p2, k2tog, yo, p2, 2/1 RC, k2, **p2, k2tog, yo, rep from ** 0 [0, 1, 1] more times, p1 [3, 1, 3].

Round 12: p1 [3, 1, 3], *k2, p2, rep from * 0 [0, 1, 1] more times, k5, p2, k2, p2, k5, **p2, k2, rep from ** 0 [0, 1, 1] more times, p1 [3, 1, 3].

Round 13: p1 [3, 1, 3], *yo, ssk, p2, rep from * 0 [0, 1, 1] more times, k3, 2/1 LC, p1, yo, ssk, p1, 2/1 RC,

k3, **p2, yo, ssk, rep from ** 0 [0, 1, 1] more times, p1 [3, 1, 3].

Round 14: p1 [3, 1, 3], *k2, p2, rep from * 0 [0, 1, 1] more times, k6, p1, k2, p1, k6, **p2, k2, rep from ** 0 [0, 1, 1] more times, p1 [3, 1, 3].

Round 15: p1 [3, 1, 3], *k2tog, yo, p2, rep from * 0 [0, 1, 1] more times, k4, 2/1 LPC, k2tog, yo, 2/1 RPC, k4, **p2, k2tog, yo, rep from ** 0 [0, 1, 1] more times, p1 [3, 1, 3].

Round 16: p1 [3, 1, 3], *k2, p2, rep from * 0 [0, 1, 1] more times, (k4, p1, k2) twice, k2, **p2, k2, rep from ** 0 [0, 1, 1] more times, p1 [3, 1, 3].

Round 17: p1 [3, 1, 3], *yo, ssk, p2, rep from * 0 [0, 1, 1] more times, k4, p1, 2/1 LPC, 2/1 RPC, p1, k4, **p2, ssk, rep from ** 0 [0, 1, 1] more times, p1 [3, 1, 3].

Round 18: p1 [3, 1, 3], *k2, p2, rep from * 0 [0, 1, 1] more times, k4, (p2, k4) twice, **p2, k2, rep from ** 0 [0, 1, 1] more times, p1 [3, 1, 3].

Round 19: p1 [3, 1, 3], *k2tog, yo, p2, rep from * 0 [0, 1, 1] more times, k4, p2, 2/2 LPC Special, p2, k4, **p2, k2tog, yo, rep from ** 0 [0, 1, 1] more times, p1 [3, 1, 3].

Round 20: p1 [3, 1, 3], *k2, p2, rep from * 0 [0, 1, 1] more times, k4, (p3, k2) twice, k2, **p2, k2, rep from ** 0 [0, 1, 1] more times, p1 [3, 1, 3].

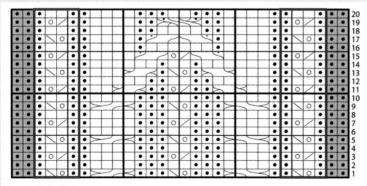

Rep 1 [1, 2, 2] times total.   Rep 1 [1, 2, 2] times total.

	Medium and Extra Large Only
•	p
o	yo
⟍	ssk

	2/2 LC	
	2/2 RC	
	k	
	k2tog	

	2/1 LC
	2/1 RC
	2/1 LPC
	2/1 RPC
	2/2 LPC Special

Nimble chart.

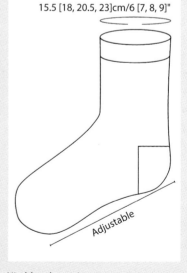

15.5 [18, 20.5, 23]cm/6 [7, 8, 9]"

Adjustable

Nimble schematic.

DEFT MITTS

Gauge

- 34 stitches by 49 rounds = 10cm [4in] in stocking stitch.
- 32 stitches by 68 rows = 10cm [4in] in garter stitch. Check your gauge.

Needles and accessories

- 2.25mm (US Size 1) needles for working in the round in preferred method for circular knitting; or size to obtain gauge.
- Stitch markers × 4
- Darning needle

Yarn

- Fyberspates Vivacious 4-ply (100g; 365m [399yds]; 100 per cent merino wool) 4-ply/fingering weight; colourway: Pebble Beach;
- 185 [205, 220, 245]m/202 [224, 241, 268]yd

Size

- Small, [Medium, Large, Extra Large]
- To fit 18 [19, 20.5, 21.5]cm/7 [7½, 8, 8½]in hand circumference
- Finished dimensions = 16.5 [18, 19, 20.5]cm/6½ [7, 7½, 8]in circumference

Special abbreviations

- **patt** – pattern: work next round of Deft chart
- **pmA/B/C/D** – place marker A or B etc.
- **smA/B/C/D** – slip marker A or B etc.
- **rmB/C/D** – remove marker A or B etc.
- **kGSR** – knit double stitch created by GSR as one stitch.
- **GSR** – German Short Row: see Abbreviations.

Deft are mirrored fingerless mitts using a simple texture pattern.

Deft uses different i-cord techniques around the cuff for a neat finish.

Techniques used

- I-cord cast-off (Chapter 6)
- Lori's twisty cast-off (Chapter 6)
- German short rows (Chapter 3)
- Picking up stitches (Chapter 5)
- Increases (Chapter 3)
- Neat knit to purl (Chapter 2)

Instructions

Cuff (both alike)

- Cast on 3 sts.
- **Row 1:** sl 3 to LHN, k3.
- Rep Row 1 seventeen more times.
- Pick up and knit 17 sts down the side of i-cord edge – 20 sts.
- **Row 2 (WS):** knit to last 3 sts, wyif sl 3.
- **Row 3 (RS):** k3, GSR.
- **Row 4:** wyif sl 3.
- **Row 5:** knit to GSR, kGSR, k2 [2, 1, 1], GSR.
- **Row 6:** knit to last 3 sts, wyif sl 3.
- Rep Rows 5 and 6 another 4 [4, 6, 6] times.
- **Next row:** knit to last st, wyif sl 1 (knitting the GSR double sts as one st).

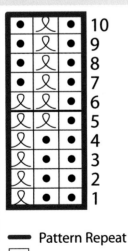

— Pattern Repeat

 p

k tbl

- **Next row:** knit to last 3 sts, wyif sl 3.
- Rep previous 2 rows another 50 [54, 59, 63] times.
- Work should measure 15 [16.5, 18, 19]cm/6 [6.5, 7, 7.5]in at shorter edge.

Note: if you find your row gauge is different, work to the above measurement. At wrist, pick up and knit 1 st into each slipped st at edge, then alter decrease round to decrease evenly to the stated sts for the relevant size.

- **Next row (RS):** knit to last 2 sts, GSR.
- **Next row:** knit to last 3 sts, wyif sl 3.
- **Next row:** knit to 3 [3, 2, 2] sts before GSR, GSR.
- **Next row:** knit to last 3 sts, wyif sl 3.
- Rep previous 2 rows another 4 [4, 6, 6] times.
- **Next row:** knit to last st (knitting the GSR double sts as one st), wyif sl 1.
- **Next row:** knit to last 3 sts, wyif sl 3.
- **Cast-off row:** *k2, ssk, sl 3 to LHN, rep from * until all stitches have been cast off. (**Note:** there should be 3 stitches left on needle).

Wrist

- Pick up and knit 52 [56, 61, 65] sts into each slipped stitch at edge of cuff, pick up 1 st from I-cord cast on – 56 [60, 65, 69] sts.
- Start working in the round (by beginning to work where the picking up started), k2tog, pass last st picked up on previous row over k2tog, pm to indicate start of round – 54 [58, 63, 67] sts.

Small, medium and extra large only

- **Decrease round:** (k6 [6, -, 5], k2tog) 3 [3, -, 4] times total, *k5 [7, -, 5], k2tog, k6 [6, -, 4], k2tog, rep from * 1 [1, -, 2] more times – 47 [51, -, 57] sts.

Large only

- **Decrease round:** k5, k2tog, (k6, k2tog) seven times – 55 sts.

All sizes

LEFT HAND ONLY

- **Round 1:** patt (starting with Round 1) for 18 [18, 21, 21] sts pmC, p1, knit to end.
- **Round 2:** patt to mC, smC, p1, knit to end.
- **Rounds 3 and 4:** rep Round 2 twice more.
- **Round 5:** m1l, pmB, patt to mC, smC, p1, knit to last st, m1r, k1 – 49 [53, 57, 59] sts.
- **Round 6:** knit to mB, smB, patt to mC, smC, p1, knit to end.
- **Round 7:** m1l, knit to mB, smB, patt to mC, smC, k1, knit to last st, m1r, k1 – 51 [55, 59, 61] sts.
- Rep Rounds 6 and 7 another 3 [3, 3, 4] times – 57 [61, 65, 69] sts.
- **Next Round:** rep Round 6 once more.

RIGHT HAND ONLY

- **Round 1:** k28 [32, 33, 35], pmB, patt for 18 [18, 21, 21] sts, pmC, p1.
- **Round 2:** knit to mB, smB, patt to mC, smC, p1.
- **Rounds 3 and 4:** rep Round 2 twice more.
- **Round 5:** k1, m1l, knit to mB, smB, patt to mC, smC, p1, m1r – 49 [53, 57, 59] sts.
- **Round 6:** knit to mB, smB, patt to mC, smC, p1, knit to end.
- **Round 7:** k1, m1l, knit to mB, smB, patt to mC, smC, p1, knit to last st, m1r – 51 [55, 59, 61] sts.
- Rep Rounds 6 and 7 another 3 [3, 3, 4] times – 57 [61, 65, 69] sts.
- **Next round:** rep Round 6 once more.

Thumb gusset

Note: If markers aren't mentioned, just slip them as you come to them.

Left hand only

- **Round 1:** RLI, pmA, knit to mB, smB, patt to mC, smC, p1, knit to last st, pmD, LLI, k1 – 59 [63, 67, 71] sts.
- **Round 2:** knit to mB, smB, patt to mC, smC, p1, knit to end.
- **Rounds 3 and 4:** rep Round 2 twice more.

- **Round 5:** knit to mA, RLI, smA, knit to mB, smB, patt to mC, smC, p1, knit to mD, smD, LLI, knit to end – 61 [65, 69, 73] sts.
- Rep Rounds 2–5 another 6 [7, 7, 8] times – 73 [79, 83, 89] sts.
- Rep Rounds 2 and 3 once more.
- **Next round:** knit to mB, smB, patt to mC, smC, p1, knit to mD, rmD, place 17 [19, 19, 21] sts between mD and mA on waste yarn, mA will become new start of the round – 56 [60, 64, 68] sts.

Right hand only

- **Round 1:** k1, RLI, pmA, knit to mB, smB, patt to mC, smC, p1, knit to end, pmD, LLI – 59 [63, 67, 71] sts.
- **Round 2:** knit to mA, smA, knit to mB, smB, patt to mC, smC, p1, knit to mD, smD, knit to end.
- **Rounds 3 and 4:** rep Round 2 twice more.
- **Round 5:** knit to mA, RLI, smA, knit to mB, smB, patt to mC, smC, p1, knit to mD, smD, LLI, knit to end – 61 [65, 69, 73] sts.
- Rep Rounds 2–5 another 6 [7, 7, 8] times – 73 [79, 83, 89] sts.
- Rep Rounds 2 and 3 once more.
- **Next round:** knit to mA, smA, knit to mB, smB, patt to mC, smC, p1, knit to mD, rmD, place 17 [19, 19, 21] sts between mD and mA on waste yarn, mA will become new start of the round – 56 [60, 64, 68] sts.

Hand

Continue in the round.

Both hands

- **Next round:** knit to mB, smB, patt to mC, smC, p1 knit to end.
- Rep previous round until work measures 4cm [1½in] from thumb hole or desired length.

Left hand only

* **Decrease round:** k 5 [5, 5, 6], rmB, *p2tog, k1-tbl, rep from * 5 [5, 6, 6] more times, rmC, p1, k4 [6, 5, 6], **k8 [8, 6, 7], k2tog, rep from ** until last 8 [10, 8, 7] sts, knit to end – 48 [52, 54, 58] sts.

Right hand only

* **Decrease round:** k8 [10, 8, 7], *k2tog, k8 [8, 6, 7], rep from * until 4 [6, 5, 6] sts before mB, knit to mB, rmB, *p2tog, k1-tbl, rep from * until mC, rmC, p1, knit to last st, place marker to indicate new beginning of the round – 48 [52, 54, 58] sts.

Both hands

SMALL, MEDIUM AND LARGE ONLY

* **Next round:** (k1-tbl, p1) across.

EXTRA LARGE ONLY

* **Next round:** (p1, k1-tbl) across.

ALL SIZES

* Rep previous round of relevant size ten more times or until desired length.
* Cast off in pattern. Recommend Lori's twisty cast-off.

Lori's twisty cast-off is used at the hand for a decorative, yet elastic finish.

Thumb (both alike)

* Place 17 [19, 19, 21] sts from waste yarn on to needles, pick up and k3 from top of thumb hole – 20 [22, 22, 24] sts.
* **Round 1:** (k1-tbl, p1) across.
* Rep Round 1 ten more time or desired length.
* Cast off in pattern. Recommend Lori's twisty cast-off.
* Darn in all ends. Use ends at thumb to darn any holes closed and block.

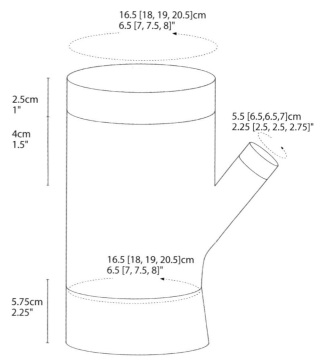

Deft schematic.

DAPPER SPRUCE COWL

Yarn

- Fyberspates Stolen Stitches Nua Sport (50g; 140m [153yds]; 60 per cent Merino Wool, 20 per cent Yak, 20 per cent Linen) sportweight;
- MC: 9810 Kitten Fluff; Light Grey; 280m [307yds]
- CC1: 9812 Cafe Flamingo; Magenta; 236m [259yds]
- CC2: 9809 August Storms; Dark Grey; 242m [265yds]

Size

- One size
- Circumference = 42cm (16½in)
- Length = 137cm (54in)

Gauge

- 22 stitches by 30 rounds = 10cm (4in) in stocking stitch.
- 24 stitches by 36 rounds = 10cm (4in) in pattern. Check your gauge.

Needles and accessories

- 4 mm (US Size 6) – 40cm (16in) circular needles; or size to obtain gauge.
- Stitch markers × 7
- Darning needle

Special abbreviations

- **MC** – main colour
- **CC1/2** – contrast colour 1/2
- **pmA/B/C** – place marker A/B/C
- **smA/B** – slip marker A/B
- **mA/B/C** – marker A/B/C
- **rmB** – remove marker B
- **LT** – Left Twist: slip 2 stitches knitwise one at a time, slip both back to the left-hand needle (without altering their orientation). Knit into the back of the second stitch on the needle without dropping from left-hand needle and knit both stitches together through the back loops.

Dapper Spruce is long cowl featuring texture and stripes. You can use the helical knitting technique on the single stripes.

Consider using your lightest colour for the textured section to let the texture pattern shine.

- **RT** – Right Twist: knit 2 stitches together without dropping from left-hand needle, knit the first stitch only and drop both from left-hand needle.
- **BOR** – beginning of the round.

Techniques used

- Provisional cast-on (Chapter 2)
- Grafting (Chapter 5)
- Jogless stripes (Chapter 4)
- Helical stripes (Chapter 4)
- Blocking (Chapter 7)

Instructions

- Using waste yarn and a provisional cast-on, cast on 92 sts. Distribute sts equally across needles as you prefer and join for working in the round, being careful not to twist. Place marker to indicate BOR.

Note: If using a provisional technique that has CC1 on the needles, rather than the waste yarn, then omit Row 1 of Wide Stripes.

Wide stripes

- **Row 1:** using CC1, knit.
- **Round 2:** join for working in the round and using CC1, knit.
- **Rounds 3–5:** using CC2, knit (3 rounds total).
- **Rounds 6–8:** using CC1, knit (3 rounds total).
- Rep Rounds 3–8 until work measures 18cm (7in) ending with a Round 8.

Single stripes

Note: consider using the helical knitting method.

- **Round 1:** using CC2, knit.
- **Round 2:** using CC1, knit.
- Rep Rounds 1 and 2 until work measures 53.5cm (21in) ending with a Round 1.

Note: If using helical knitting, finish both CC1 and CC2 at BOR by finishing with CC2 and then slipping stitches until reaching CC1, then knit to the end of round.

DAPPER SPRUCE CHART

Round 1 and all odd number rows: k10.
Round 2: k2, p6, k2.
Rounds 3–6: rep Rounds 1 and 2 twice more.
Round 8: k1, RT twice, LT twice, k1.
Round 10: RT twice, k2, LT twice.
Round 12: p3, k4, p3.
Rounds 13–16: rep Rounds 11 and 12 twice more.
Round 18: LT twice, k2, RT twice.
Round 20: k1, LT twice, RT twice, k1.

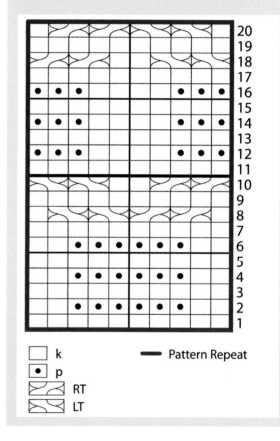

	k
•	p
RT	
LT	

— Pattern Repeat

Fade

Note: within this section, only Rounds 1–10 of Dapper Spruce chart are repeated.

- **Round 1:** using MC throughout, *k18, pmA, work Round 1 of Dapper Spruce chart once, pmB, k18, pmC, rep from * once more.
- **Round 2:** *knit to mA, smA, rep next round of Dapper Spruce chart until mB, knit to mC, rep from * once more.
- **Rounds 3–10:** rep Round 2 eight more times.
- **Round 11:** *knit to 5 sts before mA, pmA (remove the original mA when you get to it), rep Round 1 of Dapper Spruce chart until mB, rmB, continue chart for 5 more sts, pmB, knit to mC, rep from * until end.
- **Rounds 12–20:** rep Round 2 nine more times.

Note: only rep Rounds 1–10 of Dapper Spruce chart, start at Round 1 of chart for Round 21.

- **Rounds 21–29:** Rep Rounds 11–19 once.
- **Round 30:** *knit to mA, m1, smA, rep next round of Dapper Spruce chart until mB, smB, m1, knit to mC, rep from * until end – 96 sts.
- **Rounds 31–40:** rep Rounds 21–30 once – 100 sts.
- Remove mA, B and C. Keep BOR marker.

Dapper Spruce full

- Starting with Round 1 of Dapper Spruce chart, work Rounds 1–20 (repeating across the round). Rep Rounds 1–20 five more times.
- Rep Rounds 1–10 once more.
- **Next round:** k6, k2tog, (k10, k2tog) seven times, k8 – 92 sts.

Wide stripes

- **Rounds 1–3:** using CC2, knit (3 rounds total).
- **Rounds 4–6:** using CC1, knit (3 rounds total).
- Rep Rounds 1–6 until work measures 137cm (54in) or until desired length, ending with a Round 3.

The length of Dapper Spruce is adjustable, and it can be worn in a single or doubled loop.

Finishing

Darn in all ends. Place stitches on waste yarn and block.

Place the stitches from the provisional cast-on edge onto a second set of needles. Return stitches from waste yarn to needles and slip 46 stitches from the cast-off edge to move the needle tips around – this will create a Möbius loop once grafted and allows the cowl to lie flat under a coat. If you prefer an untwisted loop, don't slip the stitches. Make sure there is no extra twist in the cowl. Using a darning needle and CC2, graft the stitches together using Kitchener stitch.

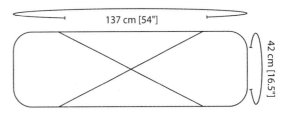

137 cm [54"]

42 cm [16.5"]

Dapper Spruce schematic.

ABBREVIATIONS

- GSR – German Short Row, see Chapter 3.
  - Right Side – When GSR is worked at the end of a right-side row, knit stitch, turn work, slip stitch to right-hand needle, take yarn directly over the top of the needle and to the reverse of the work and pull tight to draw the stitch onto the needle giving a double stitch. Bring yarn back between needles to the front of the work to continue.
  - Wrong Side – When GSR is worked at the end of a wrong-side row, purl stitch, turn work, bring yarn to the front between needles, slip stitch to right-hand needle, take yarn directly over the top of the needle and to the reverse of the work and pull tight to draw the stitch onto the needle giving a double stitch.
- k – knit
- k-tbl – knit through the back loop
- k2tog – knit 2 stitches together
- k2togtbl – knit 2 stitches together through the back loops
- LHN – left-hand needle
- LLI – left-leaning increase, see Chapter 3
- m1l – make one left: insert left-hand needle under the strand between needles from front to back and knit through the back loop (this will be tight because the strand needs to be twisted), see Chapter 3.

- m1r – make one right: insert left-hand needle under the strand between needles from back to front and knit through the front loop (this will be tight because the strand needs to be twisted), see Chapter 3.
- p – purl
- pm – place marker
- p2tog – purl 2 stitches together
- sl – slip purlwise
- sm – slip marker
- ssk – slip 2 stitches knitwise one at a time, then knit them together through the back loop (the easiest method is to leave the slipped sts on the right-hand needle and insert the left-hand needle into the front legs of the slipped stitches, from left to right and then knit them together), see Chapter 3.
- st(s) – stitch(es)
- rep – repeat
- RHN – right-hand needle
- RLI – right-leaning increase, see Chapter 3
- RS – right side
- WS – wrong side
- wyib – with yarn in the back
- wyif – with yarn in front
- yo – yarnover (take yarn over the needle anticlockwise ending at the correct side for the next stitch)

BIBLIOGRAPHY

Arnall-Culliford Knitwear, *Something New to Learn About Helical Knitting* (Arnall-Culliford Knitwear, 2018)

Bestor, L. A., *Cast On, Bind Off* (Storey Publishing, 2012)

Hemmons Hiatt, J., *The Principles of Knitting* (Touchstone, 2012)

Moreno, J., *Yarnitecture* (Storey Publishing, 2016)

Radcliffe, M., *The Knowledgeable Knitter* (Storey Publishing, 2014)

Robson, D. and Ekarius, C., *The Fleece & Fiber Sourcebook* (Storey Publishing, 2011)

Sease, C. *Cast On, Bind Off* (Martingale, 2012)

Teague, Y., *Little Red in the City* (Puritan Press, 2011)

Vogue Knitting, *Vogue Knitting: The Ultimate Knitting Book*, (SOHO Publishing, 2009)

Zimmermann, E., *Knitting Without Tears* (Fireside, 1995)

Cat Bordhi, 'Slim & Trim SSK's', YouTube, (September 2008), <https://youtu.be/bMHXK3JxrJA> accessed July 2021

Lorraine LeGrand, 'Extra Stretchy, No Flare Bind Off for Ribbing, Continental (Lori's Twisty Bind Off)', (August 2013), < https://www.youtube.com/watch?v=rWS77BKk5NQ> accessed July 2021

Nimble Needles, 'The 10 best edge stitch knitting techniques', Nimble Needles, (June 2021),< https://nimble-needles.com/stitches/the-10-best-edge-stitch-knitting-techniques/> accessed October 2021

Patty Lyons, 'Ask Patty: Let the tool do the work', Modern Daily Knitting, (July 2020) <https://www.moderndailyknitting.com/ask-patty-let-the-tool-do-the-work/> accessed April 2021.

Patty Lyons, 'Ask Patty: Magic Loop Solutions', Modern Daily Knitting, (August 2020), <https://www.moderndailyknitting.com/2020/08/19/ask-patty-magic-loop-solutions/> accessed June 2021

Roxanne Richardson 'Jogless Stripes Two Ways', YouTube (July 2019), <https://youtu.ne/AWtBteWlHtM> accessed October 2021

Talena Winters, 'Right Leaning Bar Increase', Talena Winters, <https://www.talenawinters.com/bar-increase-right-leaning> accessed July 2021

Techknitter, Techknitter (April 2021) <http://techknitter.blogspot.com/2010/04/revised-unified-index-for.html> accessed July 2021

Susanna Winter, 'How Stretchy is Stretchy? Updated Comparison of 20 Stretchy Bind-Off Methods', Susanna Winter, August 2020,<https://www.susannawinter.net/post/updated-comparison-of-20-bind-off-methods> accessed January 2021

FURTHER SOURCES

Fyberspates

fyberspates.com

Yarn supplier. Used for the patterns in the book.

Rowan Yarns

knitrowan.com

Yarn supplier. Used for all the demonstration samples.

ACKNOWLEDGEMENTS

A book is never a solo project and I have many people that I want to thank in helping it come to fruition. Firstly, a big thank you goes to Fyberspates for providing the yarn for the patterns and to Rowan Yarns for supplying all the yarn for the samples throughout the book.

Secondly, my assistant team: my husband, Jim, and my mum, Viv. Thank you for all your support throughout the process of the book, and always.

This book would not have happened without Loraine McClean, who gave me a solid foundation in knit design.

The Crowood Press have been a tremendous support throughout.

My technical editor, Linda Brown, for turning her eagle eye to the patterns in the book.

My wonderful test knitter team for test knitting the patterns in the book – Alexzandra, Christin, Debbie, Donna, Eveline, Jane, Mari, Marie, Meaghan, Pat, Sally, Tanja, Teri, Theresa, and Tove.

My wonderful cheerleaders, friends, and fellow knitters – Dawn, Julie and Kate.

And last but by no means least, thank you to all you wonderful knitters who buy my patterns and take my classes. Happy knitting.

INDEX

First published in 2023 by
The Crowood Press Ltd
Ramsbury, Marlborough
Wiltshire SN8 2HR

enquiries@crowood.com
www.crowood.com

This impression 2024

British Library Cataloguing-in-Publication Data
A catalogue record for this book is available from
the British Library.

ISBN 978 0 7198 4159 0

Cover design by Sergey Tsvetkov

Graphic design and typesetting by Peggy & Co. Design
Printed and bound in India by Nutech Print Services - India